Child Abuse Investigation Field Guide

I0878593

Child Abuse Investigation Field Guide

D'Michelle P. DuPre, M.D.
Jerri Sites, M.A.

ELSEVIER

AMSTERDAM • BOSTON • HEIDELBERG
LONDON • NEW YORK • OXFORD
PARIS • SAN DIEGO • SAN FRANCISCO
SINGAPORE • SYDNEY • TOKYO
Academic Press is an imprint of Elsevier

Academic Press is an imprint of Elsevier
The Boulevard, Langford Lane, Kidlington, Oxford OX5 1GB
225 Wyman Street, Waltham, MA 02451

Copyright © 2015 Elsevier Inc. All rights reserved.

This book and the individual contributions contained in it are protected under copyright by the Publisher (other than as may be noted herein).

No part of this publication may be reproduced or transmitted in any form or by any means, electronic or mechanical, including photocopying, recording, or any information storage and retrieval system, without permission in writing from the publisher. Details on how to seek permission, further information about the Publisher's permissions policies and our arrangements with organizations such as the Copyright Clearance Center and the Copyright Licensing Agency, can be found at our website: www.elsevier.com/permissions.

Notices
Knowledge and best practice in this field are constantly changing. As new research and experience broaden our understanding, changes in research methods, professional practices, or medical treatment may become necessary.

Practitioners and researchers must always rely on their own experience and knowledge in evaluating and using any information, methods, compounds, or experiments described herein. In using such information or methods they should be mindful of their own safety and the safety of others, including parties for whom they have a professional responsibility.

To the fullest extent of the law, neither the Publisher nor the authors, contributors, or editors, assume any liability for any injury and/or damage to persons or property as a matter of products liability, negligence or otherwise, or from any use or operation of any methods, products, instructions, or ideas contained in the material herein.

Library of Congress Catalog Number
A catalog record for this book is available from the Library of Congress

British Library Cataloguing in Publication Data
A catalogue record for this book is available from the British Library

ISBN: 978-0-12-802327-3

For information on all Academic Press publications
visit our website at http://store.elsevier.com/

ELSEVIER Book Aid International Working together to grow libraries in developing countries

www.elsevier.com • www.bookaid.org

Publisher: Nikki Levy
Acquisition Editor: Elizabeth Brown
Editorial Project Manager: Joslyn Chaiprasert-Paguio
Production Project Manager: Lisa Jones
Designer: Matthew Limbert

Typeset by TNQ Books and Journals
www.tnq.co.in

Contents

Foreword

As a boy growing up in Iowa, I can remember each morning, before I left for school, my mother would remind me to stay away from any stranger who was looking for little kids willing to share candy or look for a lost puppy. I never encountered that person, and I honestly did not pay much attention to mom's warnings then—because, in my mind, adults like my teachers, baseball coaches, and scout leaders were nice people who always wanted to help me rather than hurt me. I grew up unafraid and unaware of the horrifying experiences some children had to withstand, and I suppose—as is probably the case for most of us—it took a real life situation to open my eyes.

For me that experience took place on a freezing, snow-covered day in January of 1983. I had been a police officer in a small Kansas community for 13 years. My previous encounters with children usually focused on vandalism and runaways, and I never imagined the nightmare I was about to encounter when I was dispatched to an abandoned airport in the rural part of our community. According to our police dispatcher, somewhere in that cold, dark place with decaying hangers and crumbling runways, an unknown male had dumped a little girl. He told the dispatcher where the girl could be found, and this would be my first experience with a crime committed against a child.

It is hard to understand how, in broad daylight, a man could pull his car into a driveway, blocking the sidewalk, and convince a 10-year-old girl to help him with directions. Unfortunately, when she stepped too close to the driver's door, he grabbed her coat collar and pulled her through the open window and onto the passenger's floorboard. How she must have trembled as she was driven some 15 miles to this dark, eerie place where she was pulled out of the car, disrobed, and sexually assaulted. Horribly injured, she was forced to stand as her abductor stretched duct tape across her mouth and wrapped a pair of panty hose around her neck. Within seconds, she fell to the freezing cold ground and was left for dead.

Since that horrific day in 1983, I continued my law enforcement career and eventually retired as a Deputy Chief. More importantly, I was able to devote a great deal of that 30-year period protecting little ones by lecturing on offenses committed against children and the strategies that could be used in an effort to reduce these terrible crimes.

I recall that during the early 1990s attitudes seemed to change, and it became obvious that the worst action we could take if a child was abused, molested, or raped was inaction. Mandated reporting developed and law enforcement officers, along with social services agencies, found themselves tossed into an arena for which many were unprepared. That led to more advanced training and, subsequently, a new approach on both county and state levels with agencies developing specialized procedures that focused on interview and investigative techniques. This was a desperately needed and necessary change, but in many jurisdictions territorial issues still seemed to continually interfere.

Today, even though most professionals in this field understand the dynamics of child victimization, inadequate procedures, and a lack of interagency cooperation still create dramatic shortcomings in the entire investigative process. Currently, agencies are being encouraged to revise their policies to include uniform and detailed procedures that promote the best practices for dealing with missing, abducted, neglected, sexually abused, exploited, or trafficked children. Model policies have been developed to include first-responder guides and checklists that emphasize a multidisciplinary approach as the recommended standard that enables law enforcement, Child Protective Services workers, Social Services, and Child Advocates to work in unison while investigating crimes against children. Without this we risk investigative oversights that could be detrimental to such a time-sensitive incident involving the life and welfare of a child.

My greatest fear is that some of us who are responsible for handling physical and sexual abuse cases may still be too complacent in our approach, thus allowing victims to slip through the cracks only to be victimized again. I believe it is imperative that we bring our experience, qualifications, skills, and resources together to create a much more organized approach to investigating these horrible crimes. Expanding on a statement from the National Center for Missing & Exploited Children (NCMEC): **Our mission is to make children safer—safer from sex offenders, from abductors, from those who would steal their childhood and even their lives. Our job is to help prevent and solve crimes against the innocent.** I believe these principles should apply to all of us.

The investigation of any form of child abuse is extremely difficult. From the moment the initial call is received, every action taken has the potential to make the difference between a successful investigation or tragic outcome. From my personal experience and those shared with me by law enforcement plus child protective service professionals across this county, the one common concern has been the lack of investigative resources. Armed with the information, knowledge, and operational resources gained through this investigative guide, one can better position themselves to respond more comprehensively and effectively when a child's life may be at stake.

It takes an incredible coward to hurt a little boy, rape a little girl, or force an unwilling teen into sex trafficking. However, I believe we would be cowards if, through our own shortcomings, we allowed those responsible for abusing children to continue down this path of destruction.

Craig E. Hill
Law Enforcement Consultant
Former Associate Director of Training and Outreach
The National Center for Missing & Exploited Children
Deputy Chief of Police (retired)
Leawood, KS Police Department

Preface

Child abuse investigations often involve multiple agencies in need of information about the case. Law enforcement must investigate all criminal cases and seek justice and often punishment for the offender(s) and protection for the child. Child protective services must investigate the case and provide assistance and treatment plans with the objective of keeping the family unit together if possible. In our experience, much of the same information is needed by each jurisdiction. This guide is intended to walk the investigator, whether law enforcement or civilian agency, through the investigation process from the initial report through court preparation and testimony. By utilizing ideas and resources in this field guide, the child is spared from numerous attempts at interviews, the investigators are spared from seeking the same information through numerous channels, and each agency gets the information and assistance needed to resolve the case. When each agency and each team member is "on the same page," sharing resources and information gets the job done more quickly and efficiently.

DuPre's Acknowledgment

I have been so fortunate throughout my personal and professional life to have had many supporters who gently guided me along the way and nudged me when I needed it. Teaching and helping others is a passion for me, especially in the areas of child abuse and sexual assaults. I am particularly grateful to those who have generously shared their wisdom and knowledge and inspired me to help others through my chosen profession: Doctors Vincent J. DiMaio, Emma Lew, Bruce Hyma, and Joel Sexton, along with the Dean of Basic Medical Sciences at the University of the West Indies, Deputy Dean Wayne McLaughlain.

To my dear friends and colleagues, Gaile Heath and Gayle Byers, your friendship since college has lasted throughout the years and your staunch support is greatly appreciated.

To Jerri Sites, thank you for sharing your knowledge and expertise in coauthoring this publication. It has been a pleasure.

And most importantly, I would like to thank my mom who has always encouraged me to follow my dreams. Her unconditional love and support has given me the strength to overcome demanding obstacles and the courage to speak for those who cannot speak for themselves.

Jerri Sites' Acknowledgments

Over the past two decades, countless multidisciplinary team members and many children and families have provided the inspiration for me to continue working to improve the system's response to child abuse. A number of professional colleagues have directly influenced me during the course of my professional life. I would like to express my sincerest gratitude to those who generously shared their wisdom and knowledge, and supported me in different stages of my career, specifically: Kim Edgar-Avery, Craig Hill, Michael Johnson, Victor Vieth, Tracy Wiecking, and Robert Wilkins.

To my dear friend and colleague, Lori Fluegel: your unending support and friendship will always be deeply appreciated.

To Dr. D'Michelle DuPre: thank you for the opportunity to coauthor this publication and for your patience and guidance in this collaboration.

And most importantly, I would like to thank my husband, Wes, and our beautiful children, Abby and Jon, for their unconditional love and continuous support every step of the way.

Introduction

1

Investigative Best Practices and the Purpose of This Guide

Every investigation is different. This guide is meant to be just that … a guide. It may not be possible to spend a lot of time on each step suggested here, but investigators know that there are certain steps that must be done in every investigation; these "best practices" are standards that ensure nothing is overlooked and the best possible outcome is obtained.

Child safety has long been a primary focus of child welfare. With the passage of the Adoption and Safe Families Act of 1997 (ASFA), the federal government underscored the importance of safety, permanence, and well-being in the delivery of all child welfare services, including family foster care.

It is troubling when a report of suspected maltreatment is filed regarding any child. Reports of maltreatment occur for a variety of reasons. In situations in which maltreatment has occurred, it is crucial that the agencies involved identify the children at risk and protect them from further harm. Sometimes reports may be unfounded, emerging from the complex dynamics of the home situation. This experience can be disruptive for children, families, siblings, and family members. In each situation, it is important to ensure the safety of children during the investigation process. Public child protection agencies generally have well-developed strategies for investigating reports of maltreatment of children. In some cases practices are inconsistent across jurisdictions. More guidance is often needed to inform the many agencies and jurisdictions charged with the investigation of these cases, in the process of investigating reports of maltreatment of children. This field guide is intended to assist law enforcement officers, child protective services (CPS) workers, child advocates, solicitors, prosecutors, and other agencies working together for the welfare and protection of children.

The field needs consistent, quality practices in the investigation of child maltreatment. Currently, no uniform guidelines exist for such

Copyright © 2015 Elsevier Inc. All rights reserved.

investigations, and practices vary across states and even within state agencies. These guidelines provide law enforcement and workers from various agencies with guidance that can minimize the distress and trauma often experienced by families and children in suspected abuse cases.

The guide is useful for jurisdictions already using the multidisciplinary team (MDT) approach or wishing to establish an MDT, emphasizing increased communication among those who are involved in the investigation of child abuse. The information provided is based on national standards for best practice as recommended by federal guidelines from various agencies and research conducted by experts in the field. These guidelines outline issues that should be addressed by child protection and child placement agencies when someone files a report regarding a child in jeopardy, and are based on best practices in the industry.

The field guide is intended to be a resource for anyone working with cases involving abuse, neglect, or sexual assault of children. It is designed to be a quick reference of best practices, and yet portable enough to carry in a briefcase or back of the car and affordable enough for each team member to have a copy.

We recognize that every state has different statutes regarding these topics and even jurisdictions within the same state have varying policies and procedures for handling these types of cases. However, the objectives of recognizing, reporting, and investigating cases of this nature are essentially the same. Just as every crime scene is different, every case involving a child is different. By promoting the MDT, the victim-centered approach to these difficult cases, we will help ensure that children are protected and receive the help they need and that cases are discovered, reported, and investigated properly in order to obtain solid documentation for prosecution and conviction of the perpetrator. State and national resource information are included in this guide, and a reference web site is highlighted for users to check current and updated information in their own jurisdiction.

Background and Statistics

Each state has its own definitions of child abuse and neglect, and sexual abuse statutes that are based on standards set by federal law. Federal legislation provides a foundation for state laws by identifying a set of acts or behaviors that define child abuse and neglect. The Child Abuse Prevention and Treatment Act (CAPTA) (42 USC §5101), as amended by the CAPTA Reauthorization Act of 2010, retained the existing definition of child abuse and neglect as, at a minimum: *Any recent act or failure to act on the part of a parent or caretaker which results in death, serious physical or emotional harm, sexual abuse or exploitation; or an act or failure to act, which presents an imminent risk of serious harm.* Most states recognize four major types of maltreatment: neglect, physical abuse, psychological maltreatment, and sexual abuse. Although any of the forms of child maltreatment may be found separately, they can, and often do, occur in combination. This guide focuses on each of those types of abuse as well as child fatalities, and different types of child exploitation (US Department of Health and Human Services, Administration for Children and Families, Administration on Children, Youth and Families, Children's Bureau (2013). *Child maltreatment 2012*; available from http://www.acf.hhs.gov/programs/cb/research-data-technology/statistics-research/child-maltreatment).

Reporting Child Abuse and Neglect

Who it is that is required to report suspected child abuse or neglect also varies by state. Several states have laws requiring *anyone* who suspects that a child is being abused or neglected to report it. Many states specifically designate professions that are called mandated reporters, and personnel in those professions are required by statue to report suspected child abuse or neglect. It is not possible or feasible to include a list of states and their requirements; however, the web site https://www.childwelfare.gov/systemwide/laws_policies/state/can/ offers valuable information on numerous topics including links to state resources that identify this information by state jurisdiction. Check your state for updated information. According to the National Conference of State Legislatures, "all 50 states, the District of Columbia, American Samoa, Guam, the Northern Mariana Islands, Puerto Rico, and the U.S. Virgin Islands have laws and policies that specify procedures for making and responding to reports of suspected child abuse or neglect. Mandated reporters are required by most states to make an immediate report when they suspect or know of abusive or neglectful situations."

How to report suspected child abuse or neglect also varies by state but essentially Law Enforcement is involved in all criminal cases or crimes against children. In most states for purposes of abuse or neglect, a person is considered a child if under the age of 18 years (17 in some states, 16 in others). Special circumstances may also be a factor, for example if the person is disabled in some way but chronologically older. There are also state and federal statutes against abuse of disabled or impaired persons. *When in doubt shout!* In other words, if abuse or neglect is suspected it should be reported. Some jurisdictions have a hotline for reporting. If your jurisdiction does not, report it to your local law enforcement office and to your agency that oversees the welfare of children, such as department of social services or CPS. The Resources section at the back of this guide lists contact numbers by state.

What to report depends on what you believe or suspect is or has happened to the child. The level of certainty that you must have depends on several factors. Law enforcement and the criminal side of the house require *proof beyond a reasonable doubt.* That means that a reasonable person would come to the same conclusion that you did, given the same set of circumstances. This is a higher degree of certainty or proof than is required of the average lay person. The non-law enforcement person, however, only has to have a *reason to believe* that abuse or neglect is or has happened. Persons reporting suspected child maltreatment do not have to have proof: they are reporters of the abuse or neglect and not the investigators.

Every state has statutes that define child abuse and neglect. This guide lists general categories defined in most states. Be familiar with statutes in your jurisdiction and use this guide as a general reference. There is also a section for you to record your own helpful notes and information you use on a regular basis.

Confidentiality and Protection from Liability

It is also important to point out that most states offer a reporter of child abuse or neglect the comfort and protection of confidentiality. Reports can be made anonymously. While it is very helpful to have contact information, it is generally not required. Many states have statutes that protect the reporter when the report is made in good faith, even if it later turns out to be unfounded.

In other words, when a report is made by someone who suspects child maltreatment, and, after an investigation, the report is concluded with a finding that no abuse or neglect has occurred, the reporter is not at risk for liability issues and the identity of the person reporting the incident is kept confidential.

Immunity for Making Reports

To be eligible to receive federal grants under the CAPTA, states are required to establish provisions for immunity from liability for individuals making good faith reports of suspected or known instances of child abuse or neglect.

All states, the District of Columbia, Puerto Rico, American Samoa, Guam, the Northern Mariana Islands, and the Virgin Islands provide some form of immunity from liability for persons who in good faith report suspected instances of child abuse or neglect under the reporting laws. Immunity statutes protect reporters from civil or criminal liability that they might otherwise incur. This protection is extended to both mandatory and voluntary reporters. The term "good faith" refers to the assumption that the reporter, to the best of his or her knowledge, had reason to believe that the child in question was being subjected to abuse or neglect. Even if the allegations made in the report cannot be fully substantiated, the reporter is still provided with immunity. There is a "presumption of good faith" in approximately 17 states, the District of Columbia, American Samoa, and Guam, which means that the good faith of the reporter is presumed unless it can be proven to the contrary.

To find statute information for a particular state, go to

http://www.childwelfare.gov/systemwide/laws_policies/state/index.cfm.

With permission from Child Welfare Information Gateway (2012). *Immunity for Reporters of Child Abuse and Neglect.* Washington, DC.

Penalties for Failure to Report

As of 2012, approximately 48 states, the District of Columbia, American Samoa, Guam, the Northern Mariana Islands, and the Virgin Islands imposed penalties on mandatory reporters who knowingly or willfully fail to make a report when they suspect that a child is being abused or neglected. In Florida, a mandatory reporter who fails to report as required by law can be charged with a felony. Failure to report is classified as a misdemeanor or a similar charge in 39 states and American Samoa, Guam, and the Virgin Islands. In Arizona and Minnesota, misdemeanors are upgraded to felonies for failure to report more serious situations, while in Illinois, Kentucky, and Guam, second or subsequent violations are classified as felonies.

Twenty states and the District of Columbia, Guam, the Northern Mariana Islands, and the Virgin Islands specify in the reporting laws the penalties for failure to report. Upon conviction, a mandated reporter who fails to report can face jail terms ranging from 30 days to 5 years, fines ranging from $300 to $10,000 or both jail terms and fines. In six states, harsher penalties may be imposed under certain circumstances. In seven states and American Samoa, in addition to any criminal penalties, the reporter may be civilly liable for any damages caused by the failure to report.

To find statute information for a particular state, go to https://www.childwelfare.gov/systemwide/laws_policies/state/

With permission from Child Welfare Information Gateway (2014). *Penalties for Failure to Report and False Reporting of Child Abuse and Neglect.* Washington, DC: US Department of Health and Human Services, Children's Bureau.

The Benefits of an MDT Approach

The MDT approach to child abuse has been the recommended standard for practice nationwide by federal and state agencies and organizations for over two decades. However, there still exists a vast range of utilization of the MDT approach across the country. There are some communities with well-established teams in which law enforcement and CPS routinely coinvestigate allegations of abuse, and some communities that do not engage in this practice at all but, rather, agencies conduct separate investigations, and do not share valuable information when making determinations or conclusions.

In an effort to promote best practice, this guide emphasizes the utilization of the MDT in every step of the investigation and criminal justice process, with the expectation that the professionals using this resource either currently, or sometime in the future, will utilize the MDT approach.

Expectations of the Criminal Justice Process

Child welfare agencies and law enforcement agencies should see the investigative process as collaboration not competition. The primary purpose of the investigation is to ensure the child's safety and to make key determinations affecting the child's well-being. Every effort to provide support and minimize potential trauma and disruption to the child and family should be undertaken. In cases where an allegation of a crime against a child exists, law enforcement will typically be notified by the person reporting the incident or by CPS. Some jurisdictions do not mandate cross-reporting allegations of abuse between law enforcement and CPS. However, many do and some states mandate that a coinvestigation ensue immediately upon the report being made. Whether this statue or policy is in place or not, investigators should consider putting into practice the routine cross-reporting or allegations of criminal child abuse. This will encourage sharing of pertinent information including criminal and CPS history of the family from the beginning of the investigation, as well as prevention of duplication of efforts down the road. Oftentimes both agencies need the same information from the same source, as in interviews and documents. Working together prevents child victims, families, and collateral contacts from having to endure multiple interviews and essentially multiple investigations.

Investigative professionals should also consider collaborating with other collateral child serving professionals in their community, such as educators and medical and mental health providers, with the understanding that investigative decision making will be maintained as the responsibility of the investigating agencies. This allows investigators to gather information from credible sources while ensuring support is being provided to children and families throughout this potentially difficult process. The primary purposes of investigations are to ensure children's and families' safety in the least traumatic manner possible, while determining whether or not the allegations occurred.

Law enforcement and CPS are both concerned with the protection and well-being of children. But they are required to approach it differently. Each has a distinct role and responsibility and must resolve the issues at hand. Working together for a resolution and protection of the child helps each agency succeed. CPS has the added responsibility of treatment and assistance for the family. By taking on the multidisciplinary collaborative approach, agencies must ensure that staff are knowledgeable and consistent in the application of decision-making criteria. Although CPS investigators and law enforcement carry the responsibility for making case determinations for their respective agencies, the decision-making process should be guided by agency policy and protocols and developed with input from multiple sources to ensure sound decisions.

Documentation for all investigative activities is crucial and each agency must keep its records in ways that can be easily retrieved. If and when the case moves toward to criminal proceedings or adjudication, the documentation must be consistent and parallel for judicial proceedings.

The Law Enforcement Role

Law enforcement and CPS have different objectives. Law enforcement is concerned in finding the perpetrator and bringing him or her to justice. Conviction and punishment are the goals. Therefore, the standard of proof or the evidence needed is higher than that which is needed in civil proceedings or family court; in criminal court, beyond a reasonable doubt is expected and is a higher stand of evidence than needed in the family court. Law enforcement should *always* be notified in criminal cases.

The CPS Role

In most cases CPS is charged with the protection of children and also has the objective of keeping the family unit together, if possible, while obtaining treatment and services for the family to ensure the child's well-being. Treatment rather than punishment is the objective. Family court rather than criminal court is the venue and, therefore, the standards of evidence are different. In family court, preponderance of evidence is the guide. Preponderance of evidence means the greater weight of all the evidence. Therefore, it carries a lower burden of proof. Typically, a judge makes the legal determination in these cases, based on information gathered by both CPS and law enforcement when involved.

It should be noted that roles of both agencies intertwine when engaged in the criminal justice process. This makes collaboration not just useful but a necessity in all aspects of the system.

Dynamics of Victimization

2

Victims of child abuse are boys and girls of all ages and across all socioeconomic boundaries. Every culture is affected, and there are no exceptions for urban or rural families. The dynamics of family relationships and child maltreatment are varied and complex, and directly contribute to a child's willingness or ability to disclose about their abuse.

According to the US Department of Health and Human Services, Children's Bureau Administration on Children, Youth and Families, and Administration for Children and Families 2012 Child Maltreatment Report, in over 95% of reports of child maltreatment, children know their abuser. In most instances, their abuser is someone within the family, or someone the child relies on for their basic needs and their personal well-being. Oftentimes, children love their abuser, and they would feel a sense of disloyalty or tremendous loss if they were to report the abuse.

Over the past 20 years there has been a great deal of research regarding children's disclosure of sexual abuse, which has proven that the relationship between the child and the perpetrator has a direct impact on disclosure. "In some cases, the child is dissuaded from disclosing the abuse by family members who do not believe the child and wish to prevent shame and embarrassment to the family. Most studies demonstrate lower rates of disclosure or longer delays in doing so when abuse is by a family member rather than by a non-family member" (Olafson and Lederman, 2006).

According to Olafson and Lederman, studies show that children who have supportive caregivers are more likely to disclose. In contrast, those who are abused by a family member and do not have supportive caregivers are less likely to disclose and more likely to recant, due to feeling responsible for breaking up their family. Other reasons for nondisclosure include fear of the consequences of their disclosure and feelings of love toward the perpetrator.

Most children are naturally vulnerable and seek attention and affection, often resulting in compliance in order to feel acceptance or love. Children who are abused by a caregiver may accommodate the abuse for years in an effort to maintain their relationship, protect their abuser, and

Child Abuse Investigation Field Guide.
Copyright © 2015 Elsevier Inc. All rights reserved.

keep their family intact. Fear of being hurt by the abuser (followed by threats of harm or disruption of family), fear of disappointing others, and feelings of shame and guilt will often undermine the victim's willingness to tell about the abuse as well (Lyon and Ahern, 2011).

Mistakenly, some professionals will ask children why they did not tell someone about the abuse sooner. Professionals must keep in mind that regardless of the cause of delayed or reluctant disclosure, years of extensive research shows that children tell when they are ready to tell, and they tell when they feel safe to tell. Investigative professionals must never question why there is a delay in disclosure. Understanding the dynamics of abuse may provide professionals with the answer, and there may be no explanation at all. Rather than fixating on the cause of delayed or reluctant disclosures, which implies distrust and skepticism of the child's motives, professionals must take steps to ensure the child's safety when suspected abuse has occurred, and provide the most supportive environment possible for the child to disclose within. Once the investigation ensues, it is critical that the child and their caregiver(s) engage in therapy to work toward dealing with the dynamics of abuse and that a safe, supportive, protective environment is maintained, in order to begin the healing process.

Intra-Familial Abuse

Abuse within the family by a family member is often quite difficult for the family to handle. Remember, the closer the bond between the child and the abuser, the more difficult it will be for the child to disclose abuse. It is critical in these cases, regardless of the type of maltreatment, that the alleged perpetrator is removed from the home or the child is placed in a supportive environment. If there is a chance that the family could influence the child's statement, or cause the child any discomfort while waiting for the investigation to ensue, the child may minimize the abuse or recant their statement, which will likely result in the perpetrator returning to the home. It is highly recommended that as part of the multidisciplinary team (MDT) protocol, cases where the abuse occurs within the family (including sibling abuse as well as caregiver) should be considered as an emergency, and the child should be interviewed forensically, within hours of their outcry statement, to prevent tampering or a lack of support from other family members.

It is not uncommon for children to withhold disclosure when the abuse is by family members. The child may often relate the event subtly and partially disclose saying that they do not like to see a particular person because they do not like the way they kiss them or hug them, and so on. Often as the child grows older and develops relationships outside the home, disclosure may take place. Another development may be that the offender releases one child as he or she grows older for a younger sibling.

Special challenges in intra-familial abuse cases include delayed disclosure, perceived lack of evidence, and recantation due to family pressures (Malloy et al., 2007).

Poly-Victimization

All too often, children are victims of violence, crime, and abuse. This victimization may take the form of physical assault, child maltreatment, sexual abuse, or bullying. They may also witness such events in their homes, schools, and communities. Some children suffer several different kinds of such victimization even over a relatively brief time span. These children and youths are at particularly high risk for lasting physical, mental, and emotional harm.

Children exposed to even one type of violence, both within the past year and over their lifetimes, are at far greater risk of experiencing other types of violence. For example, a child who was physically assaulted in the past year would be five times as likely also to have been sexually victimized and more than four times as likely also to have been maltreated during that period. Similarly, a child who was physically assaulted during his or her lifetime would be more than six times as likely to have been sexually victimized and more than five times as likely to have been maltreated during his or her lifetime (Finkelhor et al., 2013). This helps explain why more than one type of victimization occurs. More attention needs to be paid to children who are exposed to multiple *types* of violence, crime, and abuse.

Most research has looked only at individual forms of child victimization—such as sexual abuse or bullying—without investigating the other exposures these same children may face. A new emphasis on the study of what is being called "poly-victimization" offers to help teachers, counselors, medical professionals, psychologists, child welfare advocates, law enforcement, juvenile justice system personnel, and others who work with children identify the most endangered children and youths and protect them from additional harm.

Awareness about poly-victimization has many potential implications for those who work with juvenile victims and what they can do to identify and intervene on behalf of children who are exposed to multiple forms of violence: *Assess for more victimizations*. Children need to be assessed for a broader range of victimizations. When children are identified as victims of sexual abuse or bullying, professionals who work with them need to find out what else is going on, as these children often experience other victimizations and adversities.

During the investigation and even the forensic interview, it is important to explore poly-victimization. This will better explain the dynamics of abuse in the case, as well as future treatment needs for the child and family.

Domestic Violence

Domestic violence affects children in the home. Having a parent beaten or killed in the home traumatizes the child whether he or she witnesses the act or not. Even seeing or hearing the argument can adversely affect children. Studies have shown that a child's exposure to domestic violence is the single best predictor from transmitting violence across generations (1996 Violence and the Family, Washington, DC, American Psychological Association). When domestic violence occurs, the risk of physical and sexual abuse to children increases dramatically from 30% to 60%. Mothers beaten by their partners are twice as likely to abuse their children, and fathers who frequently beat their wives are more likely to beat their children (Strauss, M. and Gelles, R., 1990. *Physical Violence in American Families*. New Brunswick NJ: Transaction).

Children who are exposed to domestic violence are more reluctant to disclose due to fear of being in danger for doing so. It is especially important for professionals to immediately ensure children and their non-offending caregiver's safety when allegations arise in a home with a history of domestic violence. If the alleged perpetrator is also the perpetrator of past domestic abuse, these cases must be met with care, and a sense of urgency, so that the abuser does not have opportunity to intimidate or carry out potential threats of harm, once a disclosure of abuse has been made.

Children with Disabilities

The vulnerability of children with disabilities is magnified because of their increased need for dependence on the caregiver, and greater stress and frustration for the adult. Disabled children are often more isolated from peers and lack contact outside the home. These cases present special challenges to the investigative team in many areas: communication with the child, understanding the child and how the particular disability affects this child, understanding that the disability may present differently in every child, and special advocacy for the child are only some of the considerations that must be addressed. Oftentimes, children with disabilities are credible witnesses. With patient and competent forensic interviews, a great deal can be learned directly from the child. Professionals may have to rely more heavily on collateral contacts, support providers, medical and/or mental health professionals, and caregivers to provide corroborative details in an effort to piece together the information in these very difficult cases.

Cultural Considerations

Cultural considerations for alternative and folk medicine can present as possible child abuse (see Chapter 3, section on Physical Abuse). Cultural values, parenting approaches, views of law enforcement and other public agencies, and beliefs about child rearing, sexuality, and other differences may affect all aspects of the investigation. Law enforcement and child protection agencies must make every effort to reach ethnic and culturally diverse populations in their jurisdictions and encourage them to come forward to report child maltreatment incidents. It is strongly recommended that if a translator is needed for the child or a family member a professional translator is hired and a friend, family member, or other known party is *not* used.

Sensitivity in Response

Child maltreatment cases often invoke intense emotions in caseworkers, law enforcement, and first responders. The goal of the MDT is to protect the child and punish the perpetrator without re-traumatizing the child.

Children who have suffered abuse and their families are often unaccustomed to the criminal justice system and how it works as an advocate for the protection of the child. They may be apprehensive and lack confidence in the system and its protections. Family members involved in sexual abuse cases are especially prone to distrust of the justice system. Extra time must be made for families to overcome their apprehension. Professionals must work together to achieve their goals. Even a successful outcome will be a harsh ordeal, if the process is not carried out in a positive, safe, and understanding manner.

References

http://www.acf.hhs.gov/sites/default/files/cb/cm2012.pdf.

Finkelhor, T., Turner, H., Shattuck, A., Hamby, S.L., 2013. Violence, crime, and abuse exposure in a national sample of children and youth: an update. JAMA Pediatr. 167 (7), 614–621.

Lyon, T.D., Ahern, E.C., 2011. Disclosure of child sexual abuse. In: Myers, J.E.B. (Ed.), the APSAC Handbook on Child Maltreatment, third edn. Sage, Newbury Park, CA, pp. 233–252.

Malloy, L.C., Lyon, T.D., Quas, J.A., 2007. Filial dependency and recantation of child sexual abuse allegations. J. Am. Acad. Child Adolesc. Psychiatry 46 (2), 162–170.

Olafson, E., Lederman, C.S., 2006. The state of the debate about children's disclosure patterns in child sexual abuse cases. Juv. Fam. Court J. 57 (1), 27–40.

Types of Child Abuse

3

What is Child Abuse and Neglect?

> *Any recent act or failure to act on the part of a parent or caretaker which results in death, serious physical or emotional harm, sexual abuse or exploitation; or an act or failure to act, which presents an imminent risk of serious harm.*

Each US state defines the types of child abuse and neglect in its statutes and policies. Child protective services (CPS) agencies determine the appropriate response for the alleged maltreatment based on those statutes and policies. In most states, the majority of reports receive an investigation. Oftentimes, it is difficult to separate abuse from neglect. Too many times we see both when it comes to abused children. This guide is divided into categories that hopefully will make it easier for use as a reference (and not necessarily in the way *your* state or jurisdiction may have the statutes written). It is so important *to read your state statutes on child abuse and neglect and sexual abuse of a minor to thoroughly understand your state laws and the necessary elements for prosecution* and/or family services.

Child abuse is a national law enforcement, child advocate, and CPS worker problem. It is not limited to inner city, rural, or metropolitan areas. It cuts across all socioeconomic boundaries. Child abuse can take many forms from neglect to child fatalities. "Nationally, four-fifths (78.3%) of victims were neglected, 18.3 percent were physically abused, 9.3 percent were sexually abused and 8.5 percent were psychologically maltreated, and the majority suffered more than one type of abuse. For 2012, a nationally estimated 1,640 children died of abuse and neglect at a rate of 2.20 children per 100,000 children in the national population" (US HHS, 2013).

Physical Abuse

Physical abuse definition by CAPTA (Child Abuse Prevention and Treatment Act):

Physical abuse is generally defined as "any non-accidental physical injury to the child" and can include striking, kicking, burning, or biting

Child Abuse Investigation Field Guide.
Copyright © 2015 Elsevier Inc. All rights reserved.

the child, or any action that results in a physical impairment of the child. In approximately 38 states and American Samoa, Guam, the Northern Mariana Islands, Puerto Rico, and the Virgin Islands, the definition of abuse also includes acts or circumstances that threaten the child with harm or create a substantial risk of harm to the child's health or welfare.

Physical abuse is generally defined by state statute. In essence, the statute will include terminology that will define physical abuse as temporary or permanent disfigurement or impairment of any bodily organ or function, or death. In 2012, the US Department of Health and Human Services, Children's Bureau, reported the number of cases of physical abuse to children as 125,000 (US, 2013).

Physical abuse is usually considered any type of physical force that results in temporary or permanent disfigurement of the child, or any impairment of any bodily function or organ.

Corporal Punishment: Spanking

All states allow spanking in the home. Nineteen states still allow school officials to spank children, under certain conditions (http://www.businessinsider.com/19-states-still-allow-corporal-punishment-2014-3). Know what your state law says about spanking in school. For example, a spanking across the back of the legs or buttocks that leaves marks or bruises on the child's skin is temporary disfigurement. The question often asked is "when is it too much?" We look at several factors when answering this question: Where on the body was the spanking? Usually we spank children on the buttocks. How much force was used? There is a different amount needed for a 2 year old versus a 10 year old. What was used to spank the child? Usually it is the palm of the hand. And why was the spanking given? It needs to be by the parent or guardian in order to discipline the child to do or not do something. Corporal punishment is not considered physical abuse as long as it does not meet the definition in your state of physical abuse, that is, generally, as long as it does not leave marks, even temporary marks on the child, *and* as long as it is reasonable in manner and moderate in degree. It also depends on the body area of the child that is struck. It must be appropriate and not reckless or grossly negligent. In many states, it must also be administered by a parent, guardian, or in loco parentis for the sole purpose of correcting the child's behavior. Therefore, the area of the body affected, the instrument used to inflict the punishment, the amount of force used, and the age and size of the child are all considerations in the use of corporal punishment. Know your state statute and the guidelines in your jurisdiction for spanking at school. Most states do not allow it.

Investigating child abuse and neglect is a demanding task. It should be understood that someone who has had the training and experience necessary to support successful prosecution must conduct a thorough investigation—this means each member of the team from law enforcement to CPS to child advocate to medical provider, must have a thorough knowledge of child development and of investigative practices for their area of expertise. The most important aspect of any investigation is to understand the underlying concepts of investigation and in particular of child abuse investigations. Teamwork with all agencies involved will greatly facilitate the investigation and the chance for successful prosecution.

For parents who were abused as children, abuse of their own children is 10 times greater than for parents who were not abused as children (Strauss et al., 1998).

Signs of Physical Abuse (Visible Findings)[1]

- Black eyes
- Broken bones that are unusual and unexplained
- Bruise marks shaped like hands, fingers, or objects (such as a belt)
- Bruises in areas where normal childhood activities would not usually result in bruising
- *Bulging fontanel* (soft spot) or *separated sutures* in an infant's skull. (Needs medical attention immediately!)
- Burn (scalding) marks, usually seen on the child's hands, arms, or buttocks
- Choke marks around the neck
- Cigarette burns on exposed areas or on the genitals
- Circular marks around the wrists or ankles (signs of twisting or tying up)
- Human bite marks
- Lash marks
- Unexplained unconsciousness in an infant.

Symptoms of Physical Abuse (Feelings or Actions)

The child:

- Shows sudden changes in behavior or school performance
- Has not received help for physical or medical problems brought to the parents' attention

[1] From Child Welfare Information Gateway, www.childwelfare.gov/pubs/factsheets/whatiscan.cfm.

- Has learning problems (or difficulty concentrating) that cannot be attributed to specific physical or psychological causes
- Is always watchful, as though preparing for something bad to happen
- Lacks adult supervision
- Is overly compliant, passive, or withdrawn
- Is overly clingy to a particular parent or caregiver
- Comes to school or other activities early, stays late, and does not want to go home
- Is reluctant to be around a particular person
- Discloses maltreatment.

Consider possible physical abuse when the child:

- Has unexplained burns, bites, bruises, broken bones, or black eye(s)
- Has fading bruises or other marks noticeable after an absence from school
- Seems frightened of the parents and protests or cries when it is time to go home
- Shrinks at the approach of adults
- Reports injury by a parent or another adult caregiver
- Abuses animals or pets
- Offers conflicting, unconvincing, or no explanation for the child's injury, or provides an explanation that is not consistent with the injury; the explanation does not make sense in relation to the injuries seen
- Has a history of abusing animals or pets.

The parent:

- Describes the child as "evil" or in some other very negative way
- Uses harsh physical discipline with the child
- Has a history of abuse as a child.

Typical injuries in abused children include:

- Any fracture in an infant too young to walk or crawl, that is, "cannot crawl, cannot fall"
- Bleeding in the back of the eye, seen with shaken baby syndrome or a direct blow to the head
- Collection of blood in the brain (*subdural hematoma*) without good explanation and documentation of accidental injury
- Evidence of fractures at the tip of *long bones* or spiral-type fractures that result from twisting
- Evidence of skull fracture
- Fractured ribs, especially in the back
- Internal damage, such as bleeding or rupture of an organ from blunt trauma
- Multiple bruises that occurred at different times—especially in unusual areas of the body or in patterns that suggest choking, twisting, or severe beating with objects or hands; accidental injuries and falls occur on bony prominences over knees, elbows, and so on and not on the inside of the thighs or hard to injure locations

- Other unusual skin damage, including burns or burn scars, pinch bruises on ears, buttocks, penis, and so on.

Emotional or Mental Abuse

Emotional or mental abuse is about control. It takes various shapes and is often found in conjunction with physical abuse. Mental abuse is generally verbal abuse by such things as berating and belittling the child, telling them they are a problem or calling them names, and lowering their self-esteem and self-confidence over time (www.everydayhealth.com, by Wyatt Myers, downloaded June 30, 2014). The child begins to believe the things that are said. Unlike physical child abuse, emotional abuse leaves no signs of abuse (no visible injuries). It is often harder to detect and may never actually be witnessed by anyone, often taking place behind closed doors so all that is seen are the sad effects and loss of self-esteem of the child. This makes it much harder to identify and to stop. Emotional abuse can take many forms but it has the same lasting effects on children. It destroys their self-image. Other ways emotional abuse is carried out is by isolating the child, severely limiting his or her social contact with others and disregarding their need to be nurtured and loved; failing to give the child attention and even threatening him or her is emotional abuse (www.everydayhealth.com, by Wyatt Myers, downloaded June 30, 2014).

Oftentimes emotionally abused children grow to fear attention of any kind from anyone since they have not known it from their parents or family. They believe they are not worthy or good enough for friends or to have relationships. The child feels ashamed and believes they somehow deserve to be treated this way because they are worthless.

Warning Signs of Emotional Abuse[2]

Warning signs of this may include:

- A child who is unusually afraid to interact with others or talks badly about themselves; older children will often revolt and will lack self-confidence
- Emotional abuse is all about control. Often, we do not see or hear the abuse but we see the effects of it in the child through their lack of confidence, depression, and eating or sleeping disorders.

[2] From www.childwelfare.gov.

Consider the possibility of emotional maltreatment when the child:

- Shows extremes in behavior, such as overly compliant or demanding behavior, extreme passivity, or aggression
- Is either inappropriately adult (e.g., parenting other children) or inappropriately infantile (e.g., frequently rocking or head-banging)
- Is delayed in physical or emotional development
- Has attempted suicide
- Reports a lack of attachment to the parent
- Has sketchy health care, immunizations, or needs glasses
- Is consistently dirty and has severe body odor
- Lacks sufficient clothing for the weather
- Abuses alcohol or other drugs
- States that there is no one at home to provide care
- Has difficulties in school
- Has eating disorders, leading to weight loss or poor weight gain
- Exhibits emotional issues such as low self-esteem, depression, and anxiety
- Has rebellious behavior
- Has a sleep disorder
- Has vague physical complaints.

Consider the possibility of emotional maltreatment when the parent or other adult caregiver:

- Constantly blames, belittles, or berates the child
- Is unconcerned about the child and refuses to consider offers of help for the child's problems
- Overtly rejects the child
- Appears to be indifferent to the child
- Seems apathetic or depressed
- Behaves irrationally or in a bizarre manner
- Is abusing alcohol or other drugs.
  (with permission from www.childwelfare.gov)

Emotional abuse can be subtle, but once recognized, it can be dealt with in several positive ways. Almost all states, the District of Columbia, American Samoa, Guam, the Northern Mariana Islands, Puerto Rico, and the Virgin Islands include emotional maltreatment as part of their definitions of abuse or neglect. Approximately 32 states, the District of Columbia, the Northern Mariana Islands, and Puerto Rico provide specific definitions of emotional abuse or mental injury to a child. Typical language used in these definitions is "injury to the psychological capacity or emotional stability of the child as evidenced by an observable or substantial change in behavior, emotional response, or cognition" and injury as evidenced by "anxiety, depression, withdrawal, or aggressive behavior" (CAPTA).

Emotional or mental abuse is difficult to detect and often there are no telltale signs. If suspected, report it. An expert witness will likely be called to move the investigation forward and may be needed to validate that emotional abuse is or has taken place. But anyone who suspects this is happening to a child should report it to the appropriate agency, law enforcement, or CPS, depending on who the offender is suspected to be.

Abandonment Laws: Daniel's Law and Baby Moses Laws

Abandonment laws may vary slightly by state but in general abandonment is when the parent or caregiver intentionally leaves the child with no viable means of support and does not make arrangements for the well-being of the child.

(Child Welfare Information Gateway, 2013).

Infant Safe Haven Laws

Safe Haven Laws were enacted to protect the parent from prosecution with abandonment charges if certain rules are followed and for the protection and safety of the child.

Many state legislatures have enacted laws to address infant abandonment and infanticide in response to a reported increase in the abandonment of infants. Beginning in Texas in 1999, "Baby Moses Laws" or infant Safe Haven Laws have been enacted as an incentive for mothers in crisis to safely relinquish their babies to designated locations where the babies are protected and provided with medical care until a permanent home is found. Safe Haven Laws generally allow the parent, or an agent of the parent, to remain anonymous and to be shielded from prosecution for abandonment or neglect in exchange for surrendering the baby to a safe haven and if certain other conditions are met. Each state defines what it will consider as a safe haven such as hospitals, police stations, churches, emergency medical services (EMS) locations, and others.

To date, all 50 states, the District of Columbia, and Puerto Rico have enacted safe haven legislation. The focus of these laws is protecting newborns. In approximately 12 states and Puerto Rico, infants who are 72 h old or younger may be relinquished to a designated safe haven. Approximately 19 states accept infants up to 1 month old. Other states specify varying age limits in their statutes (with permission from www.childwelfare.gov downloaded June 30, 2014).

Who May Leave a Baby at a Safe Haven?

In most states with Safe Haven Laws, either parent may surrender his or her baby to a safe haven. In four states and Puerto Rico, only the mother may relinquish her infant. Idaho specifies that only a custodial parent may surrender an infant. In the District of Columbia, an infant may be relinquished only by a custodial parent who is a resident of the District. In approximately 11 states, an agent of the parent (someone who has the parent's approval) may take a baby to a safe haven for a parent. In California, Kansas, and New York, if the person relinquishing the infant is someone other than a parent, he or she must have legal custody of the child. Eight states do not specify the person who may relinquish an infant (with permission from www.childwelfare.gov downloaded June 30, 2014).

The National Safe Haven Alliance works with states to promote these laws and increase public awareness that options exist. Together, the Alliance and states work together to save the lives of innocent infants and to protect the lives of their mothers. The usual caveats to the Safe Haven Laws are that the child is no older than a specified age, often 30 days; the child must not be harmed, including: must not test positive for drugs or alcohol when relinquished; must be given to a person at the location and not left on the door step; and must be left at a designated safe haven identified by state statute. Jurisdictions will vary somewhat and will have designated locations as safe havens, usually hospitals, police stations, churches, and others. Know the laws in your jurisdiction. To find statute information for a particular state, go to

https://www.childwelfare.gov/systemwide/laws_policies/state/

Consequences of Relinquishment

Once the safe haven provider has notified the local child welfare department that an infant has been relinquished, the department assumes custody of the infant as an abandoned child. The department has the responsibility for placing the infant, usually in a pre-adoptive home, and for petitioning the court for termination of the birth parents' parental rights. Before the baby is placed in a pre-adoptive home, 14 states and the District of Columbia require the department to request the local law enforcement agency to determine whether the baby has been reported as a missing child. In addition, five states require the department to check the putative father registry before a termination of parental rights petition can be filed and many require that "reasonable efforts" have been undertaken to locate the non-relinquishing parent.

Approximately 20 states and the District of Columbia have procedures in place for a parent to reclaim the infant, usually within a specified time period and before any petition to terminate parental rights has been granted. Five states also have provisions for a non-relinquishing father to petition for custody of the child. In 17 states and Puerto Rico, the act of surrendering an infant to a safe haven is presumed to be a relinquishment of parental rights to the child, and no further parental consent is required for the child's adoption (https://www.childwelfare.gov).

Daniel's Law is a law designed to provide a safe haven for abandoned babies. Example from South Carolina's Daniel's Law: SC Code Section 63-7-40.

A person who abandons a newborn cannot be prosecuted for abandonment if he or she takes the unharmed baby to staff or an employee of a safe haven.

Safe havens are defined as hospital or hospital outpatient facility, a law enforcement agency, a fire station, an EMS station, or a house of worship during the time in which the church or synagogue is staffed.

- If the baby has been harmed in some way, the immunity from prosecution may not apply. The law applies to infants up to 30days old. *A baby testing positive for drugs or alcohol has been harmed. Immunity from prosecution may not apply.
- The person leaving the child does not have to reveal his or her identity.
- The person leaving the child will be asked to provide medical information about the baby's parents, and if possible, the name of the baby's parents. This will help the medical personnel treat the baby for any health problems.

- The hospital will provide medical care and contact South Carolina Department of Social Services (DSS). The DSS will have legal custody of the child and will place the child in a foster home.
- DSS will immediately pursue family court action to free the child for adoption.

Contributing to Delinquency of a Minor or Aiding in the Delinquency of a Minor

Any action by an adult that allows or encourages illegal behavior by a person under the age of 18, or that places children in situations that expose them to illegal behavior. Contributing to the delinquency of a minor can be as simple as keeping a child home from school and thus, making the child a truant. It also can manifest itself in more serious behavior. For example, an adult who commits a crime in the presence of a child can be charged with contributing to the delinquency of a minor, as can an adult who serves alcoholic beverages to anyone under the legal drinking age. Still more egregious is sexual exploitation, which could include having sexual relations with minors or engaging in the production or trafficking of Child Pornography (*age may vary in states that have such statutes).*

Contributing to the delinquency of a minor is a crime in some states. In states that have statutes, it is generally a crime consisting of someone knowingly persuading, inducing, enticing, or encouraging such a child or youth to engage in actions that would constitute a violation of federal or state law or a municipal or local ordinance. Enticing or allowing a child to commit a crime for an adult, or buying drugs or alcohol for a minor or asking the child to shoplift may be considered contributing to delinquency of a minor. Local laws should be consulted for applicability in your area.

Substantial Risk of Abuse or Neglect of a Minor

In some states placing a child at a substantial risk for harm, abuse, or neglect is also a crime. Typically those states will consider activities that place the child at a potential risk as being chargeable offenses. For example, driving while under the influence or intoxicated with a child in the car may be considered placing the child at substantial risk of neglect or injury. Leaving a minor child in the car on hot days, using illicit drugs in the presence of the child, or being so intoxicated as to not be able to care for the child may be considered substantial risk or even neglect.

Some states add clauses that state time frames—for example, the child is considered in imminent danger or likely to suffer from neglect within the next 30 days. Know your jurisdiction statutes and your agency policies on substantial risk behavior.

Child Neglect

At the Federal level, the Child Abuse Prevention and Treatment Act 2010 (CAPTA) defines child abuse and neglect as:

> *Any recent act or failure to act on the part of a parent or caretaker, which results in death, serious physical or emotional harm, sexual abuse, or exploitation, or an act or failure to act which presents an imminent risk of serious harm.*

Neglect is frequently defined as the failure of a parent or other person with responsibility for the child to provide needed food, clothing, shelter, medical care, or supervision to the degree that the child's health, safety, and well-being are threatened with harm by the lack of this provision. Approximately 24 states, the District of Columbia, American Samoa, Puerto Rico, and the Virgin Islands include failure to educate the child as required by law in their definition of neglect. Seven states specifically define medical neglect as failing to provide any special medical treatment or mental health care needed by the child. In addition, four states define medical neglect as the withholding of medical treatment or nutrition from disabled infants with life-threatening conditions.

Other forms of child neglect include:

- Allowing the child to witness violence or severe abuse between parents or adults
- Ignoring, insulting, or threatening the child with violence
- Not providing the child with a safe environment (supervision) and adult emotional support
- Showing reckless disregard for the child's well-being.

Signs of Neglect

- The child wears the same clothing days in a row
- The child's clothing is dirty and the child is unkempt while the parent or caregiver is nicely dressed
- The child appears always to be hungry.

Consider the possibility of neglect when:

The child:

- Is frequently absent from school
- Begs or steals food or money.

The parent:

- Denies the existence of—or blames the child for—the child's problems in school or at home
- Asks teachers or other caregivers to use harsh physical discipline if the child misbehaves
- Sees the child as entirely bad, worthless, or burdensome
- Demands a level of physical or academic performance the child cannot achieve
- Looks primarily to the child for care, attention, and satisfaction of the parent's emotional needs
- Shows little concern for the child.

The parent and child:

- Rarely touch or look at each other
- Consider their relationship entirely negative
- State that they do not like each other.

The above list may not be *all* the signs of abuse or neglect. It is important to pay attention to other behaviors that may seem unusual or concerning. In addition to these signs and symptoms, Child Welfare Information Gateway provides information on the risk factors and perpetrators of child abuse and neglect fatalities (with permission from www.childwelfare.gov).

Failure to Thrive

Children are diagnosed with failure to thrive when their weight or rate of weight gain is significantly below that of other children of similar age and gender. Infants or children who fail to thrive seem to be dramatically smaller or shorter than other children of the same age. Teenagers may have short stature or appear to lack the usual changes that occur at puberty. However, there is a wide variation in what is considered normal growth and development (http://www.hopkinschildrens.org/Failure-to-Thrive.aspx).

Failure to thrive may be caused by medical problems or factors in the child's environment, such as abuse or neglect. There are many medical causes of failure to thrive (see below).

It is important to determine whether failure to thrive results from medical problems or factors in the environment, such as abuse or neglect.

There are multiple medical causes of failure to thrive. These include:

- Chromosome abnormalities such as Down syndrome and Turner syndrome
- Defects in major organ systems
- Problems with the endocrine system, such as thyroid hormone deficiency, growth hormone deficiency, or other hormone deficiencies
- Damage to the brain or central nervous system, which may cause feeding difficulties in an infant
- Heart or lung problems, which can affect how oxygen and nutrients move through the body
- Anemia or other blood disorders
- Gastrointestinal problems that result in malabsorption or a lack of digestive enzymes
- Long-term gastroenteritis and gastro-esophageal reflux (usually temporary)
- *Cerebral palsy*
- Long-term (chronic) infections
- Metabolic disorders
- Complications of pregnancy and low birth weight.
(downloaded October 9, 2014 from: www.hopkinschildrens.org/Failure-to-Thrive.aspx)

Other factors that may lead to failure to thrive include:

- Emotional deprivation as a result of parental withdrawal, rejection, or hostility
- Economic problems that affect nutrition, living conditions, and parental attitudes
- Exposure to infections, parasites, or toxins
- Poor eating habits, such as eating in front of the television and not having formal meal times
- Problems with genes such as Down syndrome
- Organ problems
- Hormone problems
- Damage to the brain or central nervous system, which may cause feeding difficulties in an infant
- Heart or lung problems, which can affect how nutrients move through the body
- Anemia or other blood disorders
- Gastrointestinal problems that make it hard to absorb nutrients or cause a lack of digestive enzymes
- Long-term (chronic) infections
- Metabolism problems
- Problems during pregnancy or low birth weight.

Factors in the child's environment include:

- Loss of emotional bond between parent and child
- Poverty
- Problems with the child–caregiver relationship
- Parents do not understand the appropriate dietary needs of their child
- Exposure to infections, parasites, or toxins
- Poor eating habits, such as eating in front of the television and not having formal meal times.
  (downloaded with permission from www.childwelfare.gov)

Symptoms

Children who fail to thrive *do not grow and develop normally* as compared to children of the same age. They seem to be much smaller or shorter. Teenagers may not have the usual changes that occur at puberty. It is vitally important that CPS and law enforcement understand the child developmental milestones for all child welfare cases, especially for failure to thrive. If in doubt, seek medical advice.

Symptoms of failure to thrive include:

- Height, weight, and *head circumference* do not match standard growth charts
- Weight is lower than third percentile of standard growth charts or 20% below the ideal weight for their height
- Growth may have slowed or stopped.
- For various growth charts see http://pediatrics.about.com/library/growth_charts/nboysbirth.htm.

Children who fail to thrive may have the following delayed or slow to develop:

- Physical skills such as rolling over, sitting, standing, and walking
- Mental and social skills
- Secondary sexual characteristics (delayed in adolescents).

Babies who fail to gain weight or develop often lack interest in feeding or have a problem receiving the proper amount of nutrition. This is called poor feeding.

Other symptoms that may be seen in a child that fails to thrive include:

- Constipation
- Excessive crying
- Excessive sleepiness (lethargy)
- Irritability.

(NIH MedLine Plus, downloaded June 2014)

There is no single known cause of child maltreatment. Nor is there any single description that captures all families in which children are victims of abuse and neglect. Child maltreatment occurs across socioeconomic, religious, cultural, racial, and ethnic groups. While no specific causes have definitively been identified that lead a parent or other caregiver to abuse or neglect a child, research has recognized a number of risk factors or attributes commonly associated with maltreatment. However, poverty does not equal neglect and the family must have a combination of "means to provide for the child" and not in fact providing in order for it to be neglect.

The factors that may contribute to maltreatment in one family may not result in child abuse and neglect in another family. Risk factors associated with maltreatment are generally grouped into four categories:

Parent or caregiver factors:

- History of maltreatment. We often find that parents who abuse their children were victims of abuse from their own parents or caregivers. It is considered a never-ending cycle. But the cycle *can* be broken and many parents who end up abusing their children were not the victims of abuse themselves.
- Substance abuse is often a contributing factor in neglect and abuse cases. Alcohol abuse was found to be a common link in cases where abuse took place. Oftentimes, parents would spend money on drugs or alcohol at the risk of acquiring food, clothing, or shelter appropriate for the children.
- Lack of education and knowledge and poor impulse control often lead to abuse or neglect as parents may learn to justify their behavior as appropriate. Lack of understanding childhood developmental milestones and inappropriate expectations contribute to child abuse in some families. Lack of parenting skills becomes a factor.
- Age may be a factor in that younger parents may be less mature and less knowledgeable about raising children on their own. Much older parents may not be physically able to provide the type of care needed. Age of the child may also be a factor. Infants and young children, due to their small physical size, early developmental status, and need for constant care, can be particularly vulnerable to child maltreatment. Children between the ages of 8 and 15 years may be at a higher risk for sexual abuse.
- Family issues and dynamics play a role. Single parents, families in which domestic violence occurs, job and work frustrations, financial issues, and many others take a toll on parents and sometimes the lack of ability to deal with these issues may result in child abuse or neglect.
- The child may be particularly dependent if handicapped in some way, either emotionally or physically, and may require more attention time from the parent, who then becomes frustrated and angry, often taking it out on the child. Children with physical, cognitive, and emotional disabilities appear to experience higher rates of maltreatment than do other children. Children with special needs fit into this higher risk factor category as well.

Environmental factors such as financial instability, poverty, and constant relocation also play a role in the stress and frustration a parent may feel. Environmental factors also include unemployment, social isolation, and community characteristics (NIH MedLine Plus, downloaded June 2014).

In most cases, maltreatment is multifactorial and arises from more than a single factor. By recognizing possible factors, professionals who work with children and families may be better able to intervene and help to prevent child abuse and neglect.

Absent Father Connection

Studies have shown that the frequency of child abuse events in a single-parent household is nearly twice that of a two-parent household. Children living in a single-parent home compared to those living in a two-parent home had a much greater risk of experiencing some type of maltreatment overall (used with permission from Child Information Gateway downloaded June 30, 2014).

Marital Conflict and Domestic Violence

Numerous studies have discovered that in the majority of families where spousal abuse takes place, child abuse or neglect is also prevalent. Many of these same studies have also found that children who witness domestic violence are at additional risk of being maltreated and even suffer physical abuse. Some children attempt to intervene and are subsequently physically abused.

Acute Maltreatment

Acute maltreatment means that the child's injury or death is directly related to injuries suffered as a result of a specific incident of abuse or act of negligence recently occurring. Often in such cases, the child has not been previously abused or neglected. In cases involving acute physical abuse, the caretaker may have fatally assaulted the child in either an inappropriate response to the child's behavior or a conscious act to hurt the child.

Offenders in cases of shaken baby syndrome (SBS), in which a child's brain is injured from violent shaking, often cite the child's crying as the "triggering event." In cases of acute neglect, a caretaker's onetime failure to properly supervise the child may result in a fatal injury. A common example is a fatal drowning that occurs when a parent leaves an infant briefly unsupervised in a bathtub. Far too often, children sustain fatal gunshot wounds when caretakers fail to properly secure loaded firearms. Some states have statutes that specifically assign criminal responsibility to an individual who makes a firearm accessible to a child, either intentionally or through failure to properly secure the weapon. The penalty for this crime may be increased if the child's possession of the firearm results in either injury or death of the child or another.

Chronic Maltreatment Cases

Chronic maltreatment is considered anything over 72 h and/or abuse that has been over a long period of time and is now being reported. In chronic maltreatment cases, the child's injury or death is directly related to injuries caused by abuse and/or neglect occurring over an extended period. Battered child syndrome is an example of chronic physical abuse. Although the direct cause of death in a battering case is usually a single specific injury (often brain trauma), numerous indications of previous maltreatment—old and new injuries and possible signs of neglect—are usually present. Depriving a child of food for a significant period of time is a common form of chronic physical neglect. In cases of chronic abuse or neglect, a history of the child's previous maltreatment often will appear in either CPS or medical records. Radiographs often show numerous old and healing fractures. In far too many cases, children who die of abuse or neglect have had prior or current contact with a CPS agency.

Child Fatality/Homicide

For children and babies who die, there must be a clearly documented medical history or clear evidence of accidental trauma. Every fatality involving a baby or child should have an autopsy performed by a forensic pathologist. Medical advances over the past 30 or so years have greatly improved the diagnostic capability of physicians in general and for medical examiners/forensic pathologists. Crime scene and forensic technology has also greatly advanced and law enforcement has greater capability to investigate suspicious deaths and the scene in which they are found. Cause of death and therefore manner of death can now be determined with much greater accuracy even though the perpetrator may not be known. Having this capability strongly enhances the chances of determining what happened. Strong collaboration among CPS, law enforcement, and medical professionals is essential to the case and to protection of the child or children involved.

Children typically die in one of four ways:

1. Natural death with an extensive well-documented medical history.
2. Sudden unexplained infant deaths (SUIDS) or expected death (SIDS) designated after a thorough death investigation and scene reconstruction.
3. Accident with a thorough investigation (motor vehicle, house fire, and so on)
4. Child abuse or neglect:
   a. Chronic long-term abuse where there may be a history of injuries and current injuries in various stages of healing.
   b. A single explosive incident where the caregiver loses his or her temper and lashes out at the child leading to severe injury or death. This type of scenario often shows massive head trauma or severe abdominal trauma leading to significant internal injuries.

1. Natural deaths of babies and children should be relatively easy to confirm. Birth records and medical histories will be of utmost importance. A pediatrician will be able to determine if the history is significant enough to be the cause of death and can guide the investigation and assist the medical examiner and coroner to the appropriate conclusion.
2. SUIDS and SIDS are sudden unexplained infant death syndrome and sudden infant death syndrome, respectively. These are very specific causes of death with narrow guidelines to be used to classify the cause of death in the infant as either SUIDS or SIDS. By definition, SIDS should be used as a cause of death only after a thorough examination of the death scene, a review of the clinical history, and performance of an autopsy fail to find an explanation for the death. Yet, we know that some SUID cases are not investigated and, when they are, investigation data are not collected and reported consistently. The Sudden Unexplained Infant Death Investigation Reporting Form (SUIDIRF) was designed to assist investigative agencies to better understand the circumstances and factors contributing to unexplained infant deaths. The 2006 Sudden Unexplained Infant Death Investigation Reporting Form replaces the 1996 Reporting Form. The SUIDIRF was developed to establish a standard death scene investigation protocol for the investigation of all sudden, unexplained infant deaths.

Some deaths that would have been classified as SIDS before 1999 are now being classified as accidental suffocation or unknown cause, suggesting that reporting practices have changed. Inconsistent practices in investigation and cause-of-death determination hamper the ability to monitor national trends, ascertain risk factors, and design and evaluate programs to prevent these deaths. To standardize investigations of, and reports on, the causes of sudden infant deaths, the Centers for Disease Control and Prevention (CDC) collaborated with a number of organizations to (1) revise the 1996 Sudden Unexplained Infant Death Investigation Reporting Form and (2) develop a training curriculum and materials for investigators of infant deaths. CDC disseminated the reporting form and conducted train-the-trainer classes throughout the USA (www.CDC.gov SUIDS/SIDS, downloaded January 2014).

SUIDs are related to biological, environmental, and behavioral factors acting together or separately. Undetected biological factors within infants (e.g., cardiac and brain abnormalities) can lead to SUIDs. Factors in infants' environments (e.g., soft bedding and cigarette smoke) that can be modified may be involved in these deaths as well. Finally, the behavior of those caring for infants (e.g., placing infants on their stomachs [prone] to sleep) can also contribute to SUIDs (http://www.cribsforkids.org/suids-sids-resource-center/#sthash.VD9zHANa.dpuf, downloaded January 2014).

By definition, SIDS should be used as a cause of death only after a thorough examination of the death scene, a review of the clinical history, and performance of an autopsy fail to find an explanation for the death. Yet, we know that some SUID cases are not investigated and, when they are, investigation data are not collected and reported consistently. There are more than 4600 SUIDs each year.

The current leading theory is the *Triple Risk Theory*, which states that babies must be genetically or developmentally predisposed to SUID with a brainstem abnormality, must then be in a critical development period (generally between 2 and 4 months of age), and be subjected to some sort of environmental stressor (very typically sleep position provides the environmental stress). This theory has recently been preliminarily validated by a *search study run out of the Children's Hospital of Boston*. The study was conducted on babies whose deaths were classified as SIDS versus those who died of other known causes. The brainstems of SIDS babies had significantly lower serotonin and enzyme levels than the non-SIDS babies. This is a huge breakthrough, but the cause of a brainstem abnormality is still unknown and thus there are no screening tests or treatment available.

Sleep position seems to be the most important factor. The "Back to Sleep Campaign" has gained much awareness for this issue. Babies should not be placed on their stomach or side to sleep, and *every* time matters. It also seems that *breast feeding* is best, not only because of the nutritional and immunological benefits, but even in the context of SIDS prevention. Placing baby in a crib or bassinet by themselves rather than *co-sleeping* with an infant appears to be a safer bet. *Pacifiers* are now being recommended. Infants *born to smokers* and who continue to be exposed to second-hand smoke are at a greater risk. Babies who are born *prematurely or at a low-birth weight* are at an increased risk, and unfortunately there is not much parents can do to prevent this situation, but physicians should be aware of the risk and will likely monitor preterm babies more closely for respiratory problems (www.Caden'sCause.org, downloaded January 2014).

SIDS is one of the leading causes of death among infants one month through one year of age in the USA. The National Institute of Child Health and Human Development (NICHD) defines SIDS as the sudden death of an infant under one year of age which remains unexplained after a thorough case investigation, including performance of a complete autopsy, examination of the death scene, and review of the clinical history. SIDS is a diagnosis of exclusion, assigned only once all known and possible causes of death have been ruled out (www.CJSIDS.org, downloaded January 2014).

3. Accidental death of a child

The accidental death of a child may be as a result of co-sleeping or bed sharing. In such cases a thorough investigation is necessary. The bed clothing such as pillows, blankets, and sheets will not generally cause a sufficient lack of oxygen to smother the child. Overlaying is possible when the adult is obtunded or impaired perhaps by drugs or alcohol, or sleeping aids, and if the person has a large body habitus. Re-enactment of the situation may be necessary to determine the circumstances of the case.

4. Death by Child Abuse

The convincing evidence to convict in child abuse cases depends on putting the defendant in control of the child at the time of injury or death. This is where law enforcement, prosecution, and the medical professionals must work closely together. Time of death is, at best, a range that an expert witness must fully explain and be confident in the time range stated. Time of death is determined from many factors, and the totality of circumstances surrounding the death and at the scene will help determine the range for time of death. This will likely be one area on which the defense will focus.

The investigation should be directed toward looking at historical hints, social stresses, medical findings, and the circumstances surrounding the death. With a history of abuse, domestic violence and protective services and/or law enforcement involvement, a more clear picture may start to emerge. Remember that we look at the totality of circumstances when investigating the incident. From what law enforcement and protective services observes at the scene and what the medical professionals tell us about the injuries, the team should be able to piece together what likely happened. Head injuries and abdominal trauma are the most common causes of death in the single incident/explosive situation cases. In these cases, injuries often include:

- Significant head trauma
- Severe abdominal injuries
- Cigarette burns on hands, soles of feet, buttocks
- Scald burns (often associated with toilet training)
- Pattern injuries (injuries in the shape of the item used: U-shape from extension cord, burn triangle from tip of iron)
- Bruises in unusual places: back, abdomen, buttocks, inside the thighs Accidental injuries occurring on the bony prominences: chin, elbows, and knees. Unusual areas should raise suspicion
- Bruised lips, torn frenulum, bruised ears, and bruised penis or vaginal area are red flags and causes for concern.

Internal injuries may be significant but often unseen: Subdural hematoma, skeletal injuries, occular injuries (such as black eye(s) and subconjunctival hemorrhage), and petechiae. Be aware of the child's demeanor: if he or she is "different" from their usual self, less talkative, will not meet your eye or look at you, holds head down, does not talk, or appears fatigued or unusually sleepy. Internal injuries can cause children to become agitated or restless or can have the opposite effect and they may become obtunded or sleepy and unconscious. A child may be kicked in the abdomen and live for several hours; he or she may even be walking and perhaps talking a bit, before finally becoming quiet, unconscious, and dying.

Child Sexual Abuse and Sexual Exploitation

The CAPTA definition of sexual abuse includes:

> *The employment, use, persuasion, inducement, enticement, or coercion of any child to engage in, or assist any other person to engage in, any sexually explicit conduct or simulation of such conduct for the purpose of producing a visual depiction of such conduct; or*

The rape, and in cases of caretaker or interfamilial relationships, statutory rape, molestation, prostitution, or other form of sexual exploitation of children, or incest with children.

Sexual Abuse/Exploitation

All states include sexual abuse in their definitions of child abuse. Some states refer in general terms to sexual abuse, while others specify various acts as sexual abuse. Sexual exploitation is an element of the definition of sexual abuse in most jurisdictions and includes allowing the child to engage in prostitution or in the production of child pornography for profit or gain of others.

Child sexual abuse is the deliberate exposure of minor children to sexual activity. This means a child is forced or talked into sex or sexual activities by another person. Such abuse includes:

- Oral sex
- Pornography
- Sexual intercourse
- Touching (fondling).

Consider the possibility of sexual abuse when the parent or other adult caregiver:

- Is unduly protective of the child or severely limits the child's contact with other children, especially of the opposite sex
- Is secretive and isolated
- Is jealous or controlling with family members.

Signs of Sexual Abuse

Consider the possibility of sexual abuse when the child:

- Has a sudden change in personality such as becoming isolated or not associating with known friends, or becomes reclusive
- Has difficulty walking or sitting
- Suddenly refuses to change for gym or to participate in physical activities
- Reports nightmares or bedwetting
- Experiences a sudden change in appetite

- Demonstrates bizarre, sophisticated, or unusual sexual knowledge or behavior
- Becomes pregnant or contracts a venereal disease, particularly if under age 14
- Runs away
- Reports sexual abuse by a parent or another adult caregiver
- Attaches very quickly to strangers or new adults in their environment.

Society was reluctant to deal with child sexual abuse a few decades ago. Today, it is considered a serious issue. Even so, many juries have a difficult time believing that a family member, especially a parent, would sexually abuse their child. It is difficult to determine how often child sexual abuse occurs, because there is often no physical evidence, and it is kept more secret than physical abuse. Children are often scared to tell anyone about the abuse. Many cases of abuse are not reported. Abusers are usually men that tend to know the child they are abusing. The abuser violates the trust of the younger person, which makes the sexual abuse even more devastating. Child sexual abuse occurs in all social and economic classes of people. It has the same type of risk factors as *physical child abuse*, including

- Alcohol and drug abuse
- Family and financial troubles.

Abusers sometimes have a history of physical or sexual abuse themselves. A small group of repeated abusers have the psychiatric disorder pedophilia, and their preferred sexual contact is with children.

Symptoms

Symptoms of sexual abuse in children are similar to those of depression or severe anxiety and nervousness. They can include:

- Bowel disorders, such as soiling oneself (*encopresis*)
- Eating disorders, such as *anorexia nervosa*
- Body image disorders, *the child thinks they are fat* or *ugly*
- Genital or rectal symptoms, such as pain during a bowel movement or urination, or *vaginal itch* or *discharge*
- Repeated headaches
- Sleep problems
- *Stomach aches* (vague complaints).

Children who are abused may:

- Display disruptive behaviors such as using alcohol and street drugs or engaging in high-risk sexual behaviors
- Do poorly in school
- Have excessive fears
- Withdraw from normal activities.

If you suspect a child has been sexually abused within 72 hours, the child should be examined as soon as possible by a trained health-care professional. Most pediatricians, many family medicine doctors, and emergency room (ER) doctors have not been specifically trained to examine cases involving child sexual abuse. Many jurisdictions have specially trained Sexual Assault Nurse Examiners (SANE) or even Sexual Assault Response Teams (SARTs) to perform the examinations. Some pediatricians are also trained and are on call for such cases. Do not delay a medical examination for any reason. Many signs of injury related to sexual abuse are temporary. The examination should be done within 72 h of the event or discovery in acute cases. For cases of disclosure, in which the assault happened longer than 72 h prior, the child should still have a medical examination. These are considered non-acute cases, but the child and the non-offending parent will still benefit from a medical examination, even though forensic evidence may be slim or absent. There may be a chronic or long-term condition for which medical attention is needed. Often these abuse-related examinations be conducted in the course of a normal physical examination.

A complete physical examination must always be performed in acute cases, so that the examiner can look for any signs of physical and sexual abuse. The two forms of abuse often exist together. Affected areas may include the mouth, throat, penis, anus, and vagina. The doctor may also order blood tests to check for sexually transmitted diseases (STDs), such as syphilis and *HIV*, and pregnancy in females. These tests can help determine treatment.

Photographs of injuries may help to establish what happened. It is extremely important to write down symptoms due to any form of child abuse. An examination will automatically be scheduled when suspected acute child sexual abuse is reported to police or child protection agencies. A doctor or nurse specialist can be found through CPS programs. It is extremely important that the medical professional examining the child has experience in child development and trauma and preferably has had training in examining child sexual abuse cases.

Treatment

Treatment for the physical signs of sexual abuse is the same as for any types of cuts, bruises, or scrapes. The patient may need medicines to prevent or treat STDs, infections, and inflammation. Older females may receive medicines to prevent pregnancy. All children who have been sexually abused or traumatized in any way should receive mental health counseling.

Any suspicion of child sexual abuse must be reported to CPS and the police. Medical professionals, teachers, and child care professionals are required by law to make a report. Once a case is reported, child protection agencies and the police must investigate. If the report is considered true, the child must be protected from further abuse. The child may be placed with a non-abusing parent, another relative, or a foster home (NIH MedLine Plus downloaded June 2014).

Myths Uncovered

There are many myths surrounding sexual abuse. The intent of this section is to debunk those myths and afford the opportunity for a better understanding of the crime and the perpetrator. This will help investigators, counselors, therapists, and medical professionals assist the victim in beginning the recovery process and in recognizing what may be the child's coping strategy.

The dynamics of child sexual abuse are multifaceted. Often, the child sexual abuse accommodation syndrome is seen in the victim. This syndrome is identified by the acronym SHEDR, which stands for secrecy, helplessness, entrapment and accommodation, delayed or unconvincing disclosure, and retraction. This is not a diagnosis but rather a description of behaviors the child may exhibit and may be the child's way of coping with the event (from ChildFirst Forensic Interview Training).

Myth: Since it was not reported when it happened, it can not be true. Or he/she is only reporting it now because he/she is upset and getting revenge for something else, and so on. The bottom line is that the vast majority of cases, over 80%, go unreported (NIJ, 2003). Studies have shown that 70% of abused children are told to keep it a secret (Berliner and Conte, 1990), and nearly 50% do not disclose during a formal interview. This does not mean it did not happen! In one study (Pipe et al., 2007) researchers found that one-third of school-aged children delayed disclosure for 6 months or more.

We also know that children are afraid to disclose for many reasons. The offender may be family member or someone close to the family. The child fears negative consequences from telling (Goodman-Brown et al., 2003). Children feel trapped and helpless. If it was an adult that is the offender they may not trust another adult. If the abuse has been going on for a long time, the child may not know it was inappropriate at first and therefore began to accommodate the offender for safety and coping strategies. Now the offender makes the child feel guilty and a party to the act. The offender is likely an adult. The child may not think they will be believed or may not trust another adult since the offender is adult.

Myth: The child recanted or retracted the statement therefore it must not have happened.

We know that child recantation rates can be as high as 50%. This does not mean that it was not true. Children recant for many reasons: fear is a strong motivator. The child or the child's family (even a pet) may have been threatened. Also, for many children, fear of the unknown is too scary. The child may be threatened to be removed from the family and placed in an unknown environment unable to see siblings and the non-offending parent.

Myth: He/she did not report it when it happened therefore the child is making it up now for retaliation or response to some parental discipline.

Children may not report the incident when it happens for many reasons: they may not know it is wrong or inappropriate. They may not have known that it was inappropriate when it began and now they do know but are told it's "too late because they have been a willing participant" according to the offender.

Children also play a blame-shame game with themselves. They often blame themselves for things adults do. We see this in families who are going through a divorce. The child may believe it is his or her fault. Or may say to themselves, for example, "If only I were a better little girl, this wouldn't happen to me."

We know that having a nonsupportive mother can hinder the child from disclosing or intimidate the child into recantation once abuse has been disclosed.

Another reason children may not disclose at the time of the event or may recant later is that they still have a relationship with the offender; he or she is still a family member and regardless of the treatment the child may still love the individual. The non-offending parent may intimidate the child into not telling.

Each child and each family situation is different and there may be numerous other reasons a child does not initially disclose or chooses to recant at a later time. Do not assume that the child's statement was not true. Remember the dynamics of victimization can be wide and varied. Disclosure of sexual abuse is a process not an event (Sorenson and Snow, 1991).

Investigating Sexual Assaults: Medical Issues

STDs comprise a wide range of infections and conditions that are transmitted mainly by sexual activity. The classic STDs, gonorrhea and syphilis, are now being overshadowed by a new set of STDs that are not only more common, but are also more difficult to diagnose and treat. These new STDs include infections caused by *Chlamydia trachomatis* (chlamydia), human papilloma virus (HPV), bacterial vaginosis (BV), and human immunodeficiency virus (HIV). Rapid application of new technology to the diagnosis of STDs has led to a growing array of diagnostic laboratory tests that require critical evaluation by clinicians and a critical review by law enforcement.

Accurate information about STDs in victims of sexual abuse has been hindered by a variety of factors:

- The prevalence of sexually transmitted infections may vary regionally and among different populations within the same region.
- In older adolescents and teenagers, few studies have attempted to differentiate between infections existing prior to sexual abuse and those that result from abuse. The presence of a preexisting infection in adults is usually related to prior sexual activity. In children, however, preexisting infections may be related to prolonged colonization after perinatal acquisition through vertical transmission. But there should be well-documented medical records to substantiate that claim.
- Acquisition immediately before and after birth, inadvertent nonsexual spread, prior peer sexual activity, or prior sexual abuse could all be explanations for the infection.
- The incubation periods for STDs range from a few days for gonorrhea to several months for HPV. *The incubation periods and the timing of an examination after an episode of abuse are critically important in detecting infections.*

When presented with a child with an STD, attempts must be made to determine unequivocally if the infection was associated with sexual contact and, for the purposes of prosecution, whether appropriate diagnostic methods were used. The following facts should be kept in mind:

- STDs may be transmitted during sexual assault but certain STDs can be obtained in other ways.
- Multiple episodes of abuse increase the risk of STD infection, probably by increasing the number of contacts with an infected individual, and rates of infection also vary by the type of assault. For example, vaginal or rectal penetration is more likely to lead to detectable STD infection than fondling.
- Sexual assault is a violent crime that affects children of all ages, including infants.
- The majority of children who are sexually abused will have no physical complaints related either to trauma or to STD infection. Most sexually abused children do not indicate that they have genital pain or problems. Often there is no physical evidence of sexual contact, mostly because the report is made much later than the actual assault.
- In children the isolation of a sexually transmitted organism may be the first indication that abuse has occurred.
- In most cases, the site of infection is consistent with a child's history of assault.
- Although the presence of a sexually transmissible agent in a child over the age of 1 month is suggestive of sexual abuse, exceptions do exist. Rectal and genital chlamydial infections in young children may be due to a persistent perinatally acquired infection, which may last for up to 3 years. The incidence and prevalence of sexual abuse in children are difficult to estimate.
- Most sexual abuse in childhood escapes detection for quite some time.
- Patterns of childhood sexual abuse appear to depend on the sex and age of the victim.
- Between 80% and 90% of sexually abused children are female (average age: 7–8 years).
- Between 75% and 85% of sexually abused children were abused by a male assailant, an adult or minor known to the child. This individual is most likely a family member such as the father, stepfather, mother's boyfriend, or an uncle or other male relative.
- Victims of unknown assailants tend to be older than children who are sexually abused by someone they know and are usually only subjected to a single episode of abuse.
- Sexual abuse by family members or acquaintances usually involves multiple episodes over periods ranging from 1 week to years.
- Most victims describe a single type of sexual activity, but over 20% have experienced more than one type of forced sexual act. Vaginal penetration has been reported to occur in approximately one-half and anal penetration in one-third of female victims of sexual abuse.
- Over 50% of male victims of sexual abuse have experienced anal penetration.

- Other types of sexual activity, including oral-genital contact and fondling, occur in 20–50% of victims of sexual abuse.
- Children who are sexually abused by known assailants usually experience less physical trauma, including genital trauma, than victims of assaults by strangers because such trauma might arouse suspicion that abuse is occurring. Because the child knows the offender, they may be less likely to complain or disclose information.

Common Mistakes Investigators Make

One of the most common mistakes investigators make is believing that if the child recants a statement or refuses to give a statement, that the event did not occur. We know that children recant or fail to disclose for many reasons. The most common is fear; fear of losing their loved one (yes, even though that may be the very person who has abused them), fear of rejection by family members, fear of not being believed, fear for the family from threats of violence from the offender, guilt, and self-blame, and many others.

Another mistake that is often made is to not interview siblings in the household. Children are really prone to tell the truth. Often, disparities in the stories of adults are discovered from the statements children tell.

If something does not "feel" right, it probably is not. Keep digging until you are satisfied that the story and statements you are getting make sense and support the evidence you see at the scene and with the child.

Drug-Facilitated Sexual Assaults

Teens and preteens may be the victims of drug-facilitated sexual assaults. The most commonly used drug is alcohol. It is legal, inexpensive, and the offender usually does not have to force the victim to drink it or do it clandestinely. Other commonly used drugs are rohypnol, ecstasy, GHB (γ-hydroxybutyric acid), ketamine, and several others. These drugs are usually colorless and odorless and easy to disguise in a drink. Often the victim is unaware and does not remember the hours before. We know that the victim does not have to be on a planned date. These assaults may take place at any time or place and be perpetrated by friends, acquaintances, or even family members. If drugs are a possibility, a drug screen should take place as quickly as possible since many of these may leave the system within hours.

Sexual Exploitation and Trafficking

Sexual exploitation of children can be done commercially or by someone the child knows. If a person travels overseas or in the USA for sex with minors it may be considered sexual exploitation. The average age of a commercially sexually exploited child is 12, 3 years younger than it was 10 years ago and the trend is getting younger.

Other examples include:

- Internet crimes against children
- Engages in the sex trafficking of children.

Sexual exploitation of a child is traumatic sexualization and betrayal, and is damaging to the child's development. It leaves the child powerless and stigmatized.

Child Pornography and Internet Crimes

Project iGuardian, a partnership with the community and the Office of Immigration Customs Enforcement (ICE) (downloaded from http://www.ice.gov/cyber-crimes/iguardian.htm) helps kids, teens, and parents be smart about online safety and stay safe from online sexual predators. Cybercrime is the fastest growing area of crime as more criminals seek to exploit the speed, convenience, and anonymity that the Internet provides to commit a diverse range of criminal activities. Today's online crime includes attacks against computer data and systems, identity theft, distribution of child pornography, penetration of online financial services, using social networks to commit crimes, and the deployment of viruses, along with email scams such as phishing. Symantec's 2012 Norton Cybercrime Report stated that the world spent an estimated $110 billion to combat cybercrime, an average of nearly $200 per victim. The investigation is often further complicated because of the technology itself. Savvy Internet users can reroute their IP address through numerous sites leading investigators on a wild goose chase. Then, when investigators are able to locate the perpetrator, he or she may be several jurisdictions away and out of reach through neighboring jurisdictions and MOUs (memoranda of understanding), MOA (Memorandum of Agreement).

Law enforcement agencies and corporate security officers around the world with the responsibility for enforcing, investigating, and prosecuting cybercrime are overwhelmed, not only by the sheer number of crimes being committed but by a lack of adequate training. The Office of Juvenile Justice and Delinquency Prevention (OJJDP) has become proactive in developing a nationwide response to addressing these issues. Through OJJDP, there exists an Internet Crimes Against Children (ICAC) Task Force in each state, which, when notified, will either assist or investigate these sensitive, complicated crimes. The task forces consist of highly trained investigators who have access to technology and resources that enable competent and thorough investigations. The ICAC Task Forces provide technical assistance and training as well. Each state's ICAC Task Force contact information can be found at

https://www.icactask force.org/Pages/TaskForceContactInfo.aspx.

The National Center for Missing and Exploited Children (NCMEC) serves as another valuable resource in investigating child pornography and Internet crimes. "Child sexual exploitation is a significant problem requiring a multifaceted response. The National Center for Missing and Exploited Children works with federal, state and local law enforcement in their efforts to investigate and prosecute these cases and identify and rescue child victims." http://missingkids.org/exploitation.

The organization provides assistance to law enforcement in their efforts to locate noncompliant sex offenders in the USA through the Sex offender Tracking Team, as well as analytical services to law enforcement in their investigations of child sex trafficking through the Child Sex Trafficking Team.

NCMEC's CyberTipline is operated in partnership with the Federal Bureau of Investigation (FBI), Immigration and Customs Enforcement, US Postal Inspection Service, US Secret Service, military criminal investigative organizations, US Department of Justice, Internet Crimes Against Children Task Force program, and other state and local law enforcement agencies. Reports to the CyberTipline are made by the public and electronic service providers (ESPs). The ESPs are required by law to report apparent child pornography to law enforcement via the CyberTipline (18 USC 2258A).

Reports are continuously triaged to help ensure children in imminent danger get first priority. Analysts review reports and

- Examine and evaluate the content
- Add related information that may be useful to law enforcement
- Use publicly available search tools to determine the geographic location of the apparent criminal act
- Provide all information to the appropriate law enforcement agency for potential investigation.

The CyberTipline reporting mechanism assists law enforcement and prosecutors in their detection, investigation, and prosecution of child sexual exploitation crimes. The CyberTipline help make law enforcement's efforts more efficient and maximizes the limited resources available in the fight against child sexual exploitation. The value of the CyberTipline as a source of leads for law enforcement has been greatly enhanced by collaboration with ESPs. In addition to referring CyberTipline reports to law enforcement for potential investigation, the NCMEC engages with the Internet industry on voluntary initiatives to reduce child sexual exploitation online, http://missingkids.org/CyberTipline.

NCMEC's CVIP (Center for Violence and Injury Prevention) was launched in 2002 after NCMEC analysts repeatedly saw images of the same child victims in their reviews and began tracking which victims had been previously identified by law enforcement. The project became more significant after the Supreme Court held that the criminalization of child pornography applies only to images depicting "real" children (*Ashcroft v. Free Speech Coalition*, 535 US 234 (2002)). Today CVIP operates with a dual mission. The program assists federal and state law enforcement agencies and prosecutors with child pornography investigations, and assists law enforcement in identifying child victims so they can locate and rescue them from exploitive situations. The process involves law enforcement officers submitting copies of seized child pornography images to federal law enforcement agents colocated at NCMEC. CVIP analysts review the copies of the seized images and videos and determine which images contain previously identified child victims. Through June 2014 analysts have reviewed more than 115 million images and videos. Many children have been rescued from ongoing exploitation as a result of CVIP's assistance to law enforcement. For more information about other services, how to submit images for review, how to submit new case information, or how to request assistance, law enforcement agencies can contact CVIP at cvip@ncmec.org (from http://missingkids.org/CVIP).

- "Exploit" means to use unfairly for one's own advantage. For example, photographing the child in a compromising situation, with the intent to either:
  - use the photos for their own sexual stimulation or
  - to sell the photos as pornography
  - possess, trade or produce child pornography
- "Exploit" can also mean kidnapping and selling children into prostitution.

Commercial sexual exploitation of children may include:

1. Drug facilitator
2. Computer-assisted family sexual exploitation
3. Adult trafficking connection
4. Call operations (call in/call out)
5. Online classified trafficking
6. Juvenile pimping
7. Gang exploited pimping
8. Sexually-oriented business
9. Placement-related sexual exploitation
10. Brothel-based exploitation
11. Mobile brothel
12. Sturgess Biker Rally (any biker rally)
13. Survival sex (runaway)
14. Cyber enticement
15. Street trafficking or "hooking."

Article source: http://EzineArticles.com/212286.

- *Trafficking of children* or the *sale of children* is a form of *human trafficking* and is defined as the "recruitment, transportation, transfer, harboring, and/or receipt" of a child for the purpose of exploitation. The commercial exchange for profit, of human beings who are then placed in situations where they are subjected to involuntary acts such as sexual exploitation, forced labor, involuntary servitude, or debt bondage.
- Trafficking involves the process of using physical force, fraud, deception, or other forms of coercion or intimidation to obtain, recruit, harbor, and transport people.
- Victims include men, women, young teens, and children.
- The most used form of human trafficking involves "involuntary sexual servitude" or prostitution as we know it. This is accomplished through the use of brothels, massage parlors, pornography production, or street prostitution.

Human Trafficking Organizations are Businesses

The organization is run like a business with multiple business units and specialized responsibilities. For example, the actual names may vary but the functions are essentially the same:

- Management/supervising unit—this unit drafts, plans, finances, manages, and supervises the whole operation and maintains a criminal structure that is both operable and profitable.

- Recruitment unit— this unit advertises the organization and recruits new clients through means ranging from informal word of mouth to formal advertisements in the press, on the Internet, or via the use of travel agencies.
- Escort unit—this unit is responsible for transport from the source countries through the transit countries to the country of origin.
- Re-escort unit—this unit is responsible for "escorting" or routing trafficked persons (usually involving prostitution) between cities or countries.
- Guiding/navigation unit—this unit comprises individuals who know, and make arrangements in, the local environment.
- Supporting/logistics unit—this unit provides supporting services such as food and safe houses.
- Debt collection unit—this unit is responsible for collecting transportation fees and keeping smuggled and trafficked people isolated in safe houses.
- Exploiting unit—this unit operates in the destination country and may consist of numerous subunits in various activities (prostitution, pick pocketing, car theft, drug smuggling, or begging).

Human trafficking organizations recruit, keep, and control victims in numerous ways:

- Forced labor and/or child labor
- Young boys and girls can be used as domestics, for prostitution, and in pornographic activities throughout the world.

The trafficking organization makes money through:

- Prostitution
- Exotic dancing (strip clubs)
- Servile marriages (mail order brides)
- Agricultural work
- Landscape work
- Domestics and child care
- Factory, restaurant, and construction work
- Hotel housekeeping
- Day labor.

Trafficking versus Smuggling

What is the difference between human trafficking and human smuggling? A lot! The most apparent is the fact that the smuggled person wants to be there. The victim of the human trafficker does not. In smuggling cases, the victim leaves their homeland in pursuit of the "American Dream." The process is voluntary. A fee is agreed upon and is paid up front. If the fee is not paid up front then payment is due upon arrival in the country.

Dynamics of Trafficking Victims

A victim of human trafficking will show evidence of being controlled. There will likely be evidence of an inability to move or leave a job. There may be physical signs of abuse such as bruises or other signs of battering. The victim may exhibit signs or symptoms of fear or depression. Oftentimes the victim is non-English speaking and has difficulty communicating outside the control of the trafficker. The victim of a trafficker is usually recently brought into this country from Eastern Europe, Asia, Latin America, Mexico, Canada, Africa, or India. They have no passport, immigration, or identification documentation in their possession, even though the trafficker may have it. If the fee is not paid then the victim must agree to work off their debt (trafficking), which is the exploitation of that victim for labor or services for a debt for which they never make enough money to pay off. Trafficking is not voluntary.

The victims need housing, food, medical attention, safety, and security for themselves and their family, cash, and legal status. The trafficker promises these things and more *after* the victim pays off their debt. This keeps the trafficker in control of the victim, and the victim in a subservient position afraid to make a move against the person in control. Threats of harm to the child's family are often used to maintain control.

How Do Traffickers Control Victims?

- Beatings, burnings, rapes, and starvation
- Isolation
- Psychological abuse
- Drug dependency
- Document withholding
- Debt bondage
- Threats of deportation
- Threats against the victim's family or friends in their home country.
- Moving victims from one location to another or trading them, keeping them confused about what city, town, or state they are in; moving them along a prostitution circuit from state to state to avoid familiarity and detection by law enforcement—they may stay in a city no longer than 2 weeks to one month.
- They may also restrict the movement of the victim so they only have contact with those in the inner network circle.

The child victim may try to cope by repeatedly running away or the use of drugs or alcohol, or by self-injury like cutting (posttraumatic stress disorder, PTSD). In some cases the victim turns from victim to victimizer. There is an average 4-year age difference, and the new victimizer is often sent to recruit others.

Characteristics of the perpetrators range from very large well-organized to small mom and pop shops, often decentralized or isolated so as not to bring down the entire organization in the event law enforcement becomes aware of them.

Interviews should be conducted with other investigating agencies: CPS and law enforcement to avoid having to retell the trauma.

Law Enforcement Officer Protocol for Trafficking Interviews

- Remember that traffickers may not be easy to distinguish from victims. Victims may collaborate in order to survive.
- Educate yourself on the trauma of human trafficking, its impact, and effects on the victims.
- Have a compassionate and nonjudgmental manner.
- Conduct interviews with victims and witnesses, in plain clothes if possible.
- Conduct interviews individually and in private unless an attorney, counselor, or interpreter is needed.
- If an interpreter is needed, make sure to get a skilled independent interpreter who is in no way connected to the traffickers or to the victim.
- Do not begin your interview with a threat of documentation or legal status.
- Your first questions should not be "Are you a slave, are you a trafficking victim?" Start out with general questions about the person and who they are and where they live.
- Allow the victim to tell their story before asking if others are involved.
- Let the victim know they are safe and offer resources to assist them.

Initial Questions for First Law Enforcement Officer Interview

Explain the situation to the victim.

In addition:

- Do not make any promises to the victim.
- Establish your familiarity with the facts of the situation.
- Ask how they got into the USA and whether anyone helped them.
- Ask what did they think they would be doing to make a living in this country.
- Ask whether there were people always watching them or whether they were free to come and go as they pleased.

- Determine whether or not they have documents. If not, did someone take them away?

Also ask:

- What type of work do they do, are they paid, and how much?
- Does their boss hold their money or do they get to keep it?
- Are they free to contact their family and do they have any friends?
- Do they live and work in the same place?
- Has their boss threatened to call the authorities?
- Has the boss done anything to hurt them physically or made threats to them or their family?
- Do they feel scared where they are now?

Federal Statutes on Human Trafficking

- 18 USC §1589 Forced Labor—Threatening the victim that if they did not perform stated labor or services that physical harm would come to them.
- 18 USC §1590—Trafficking with respect to peonage, slavery, involuntary servitude, or forced labor. Meaning a person who knowingly recruits, harbors, transports, provides, or obtains any person and uses that person for labor against their will.
- 18 USC §1591—Sex trafficking of children or by force, fraud, or coercion. Meaning that a person who knowingly recruits, harbors, transports, provides, or obtains any person by way of forcing that person via fraud or coercion to participate in a commercial sex act and then benefits financially from that sex act.
- 18 USC §1592—Unlawful conduct with respect to documents in furtherance of trafficking, peonage, slavery, involuntary servitude, or forced labor.
- It is unlawful for any person to confiscate, conceal, remove, or destroy the passport, immigration papers, or identification document of the victim thus preventing them from leaving their undesirable situation.

Trafficking Victims Protection Act

- Provides information on the prevention through awareness and education
- Provides protection for victims through benefits and services
- Helps victims rebuild their lives
- Enables prosecution of traffickers
- Gives law enforcement clear-cut laws to make charges.

Resources for Victims of Trafficking

- To qualify for publicly funded services such as housing, food stamps, and health care a victim must be certified by health and human services.

- Certification occurs when a victim has been granted "continued presence" and is willing to assist law enforcement or has filed for a "T Visa" that has met qualifying specifications.

Each year, countless children around the world fall prey to sexual predators. These young victims are left with permanent psychological, physical, and emotional scars. When a recording of that sexual abuse is made or released onto the Internet, it lives on forever. It haunts the children depicted in it, who live daily with the knowledge that countless strangers use an image of their worst experiences for their own gratification.

ICE encourages the public to report suspected child predators and any suspicious activity through its toll-free hotline at 1-866-DHS-2ICE. This hotline is staffed around-the-clock by investigators.

Predators Face Severe Penalties

Several laws increase the probability that sexual predators who harm children will suffer severe consequences, including the Mann Act, the 1994 Child Sexual Abuse Prevention Act, the 2003 Protect Act, and the 2006 Adam Walsh Child Protection and Safety Act. Federal law bars US residents from engaging in sexual or pornographic activities anywhere in the world with a child under 18 years. ICE works with law enforcement agencies and advocacy groups around the globe to investigate crimes of this nature. Those convicted in the USA face significant penalties:

- Up to 30 years in prison for possession, manufacture, and distribution of child pornography
- Up to 30 years in prison for a traveling child sex offender, a facilitator of sex with children, or a participant in these crimes
- Up to a life sentence for sex trafficking children for prostitution.

Child Sex Tourism

Child sex tourism (CST) is defined as travel abroad to engage in the commercial sexual exploitation of a child under the age of 18 years. Some CST offenders, usually novices to the commercial sex trade, plan their travel through US-based tour companies or tour operators, whereas other offenders plan their travel independently. Information on procuring children in foreign destinations is readily available in pedophile newsgroups and forums on the Internet. In certain countries where there is a thriving commercial sex industry, such information can be obtained through taxi drivers, hotel concierges, newspaper advertisements, and so on. Studies show Southeast Asian countries—particularly Cambodia, the Philippines, and Thailand—are the most common destinations for CST. Latin American countries such as Costa Rica, Mexico, and Brazil are also emerging destinations for CST. An estimated 25% of child sex tourists in the above Southeast Asian countries are US citizens, whereas an estimated 80% of CST offenders in Latin American countries are US citizens. Atlanta, Georgia is a leading city for human trafficking in the USA.

The FBI's Criminal Investigative Division—of which the VCAC (Violent Crimes Against Children) program is a part—in conjunction with the International Operations Division, has implemented joint operations overseas with governments in some of the top CST destination countries in Southeast Asia. Based on the success of these operations, the CST initiative has expanded into selected countries in Latin America. These operations target child sex tourists who do not plan their illegal activities from the USA, but rather seek to procure children once they arrive at their destination. The purpose of these operations is to coordinate with foreign law enforcement to gather evidence against US offenders that is admissible in US courts, with the goal of extraditing those offenders back to the USA for prosecution. The VCAC program coordinates all efforts with FBI legal attachés in these countries to provide training, equipment, and logistical support to these joint operations (downloaded from National Center for Missing and Exploited Children).

Human Trafficking Investigations

Child sexual exploitation investigations—many of them undercover—are conducted in FBI field offices by Child Exploitation Task Forces (CETFs), which combine the resources of the FBI with those of other federal, state, and local law enforcement agencies. Each of the FBI's 56 field offices has worked on investigations developed by the VCAC program, and several of our legal attaché offices have coordinated with appropriate foreign law enforcement partners on international investigations. Many of these investigations are also carried out in coordination with Internet Crimes Against Children (ICAC) Task Forces, which are funded by the Department of Justice. Furthermore, training is provided to all law enforcement involved in these investigations, including federal, state, local, and foreign law enforcement agencies.

During the early stages of the program, a substantial amount of time was spent conducting investigations on commercial online service providers that provided numerous easily accessible "chat rooms" where teenagers and preteens could meet and converse with one another. Today, not only chat rooms but also other social networking and online media forums offer the advantage of immediate communication around the world, providing pedophiles with an anonymous means of identifying and recruiting child victims into sexually illicit relationships.

As the years have passed, the program has expanded its scope to include investigations involving all areas of the Internet and online services, including:

- Internet web sites that post child pornography
- Internet news groups
- Internet Relay Chat (IRC) channels
- Online groups and organizations (eGroups)
- Peer-to-peer (P2P) file-sharing programs
- Bulletin board systems (BBSs) and other online forums
- Social networking venues.

FBI agents and task force officers go online into predicated locations using fictitious screen names and engaging in real-time chat or email conversations with subjects in order to obtain evidence of criminal activity. Investigation of specific online locations can be initiated through:

- A citizen complaint
- A complaint by an online service provider
- A referral from a law enforcement agency
- Uncovering the name of the online location (i.e., a chat room) that suggests illicit activity.

The FBI exercises jurisdiction and investigative responsibilities pursuant to federal statutes pertaining to various violent crimes against children found in the Federal Criminal Code and Rules under Title 18 of the US Code.

The FBI has taken the necessary steps to ensure that the VCAC program remains viable and productive through the use of new technology and sophisticated investigative techniques, through coordination of the national investigative strategy, and through a national liaison initiative with a significant number of commercial and independent online service providers. To date, the program has been highly successful and has proven to be a logical, efficient, and effective method to identify and investigate individuals who are using the Internet for the purpose of sexually exploiting children.

Suspected child sexual exploitation or missing children may also be reported to the National Center for Missing and Exploited Children, an Operation Predator partner, at 1-800-843-5678.

References

Berliner, L., Conte, J.R., 1990. The process of victimisation: The victims' perspective. Child Abuse and Neglect 14 (1), 29–40.

Child Welfare Information Gateway, 2013. Infant safe haven laws. Washington, DC: U.S. Department of Health and Human Services, Children's Bureau.

Child Abuse Prevention and Treatment Act, 2010. 42 USC 5101 et seq; 42 USC 5116 et seq.

Goodman-Brown, T.B., Edelstein, R.S., Goodman, G.S., Jones, D.P.H., Gordon, D.S., May 2003. Why children tell: a model of children's disclosure of sexual abuse, Child Abuse & Neglect 27 (5), 525–540. ISSN 0145-2134, https://dx.doi.org/10.1016/S0145-2134(03)00037-1.

Pipe, M.E., et al., 2007. Child sexual abuse: Disclosure, delay and denial. Lawrence Erlbaum Associates, Inc., Mahwah, NJ, pp. 77–96.

South Carolina ChildFirst™ Gundersen National Child Protection Training Center.

Sorenson, T., Snow, B., 1991. How children tell: The process of disclosure in child sexual abuse. Child Welfare 70, 3–13.

Strauss, M., et al., 1998. Child Abuse Neglect 22, 249; from www.pubpages.unh.edu.

US Department of Health and Human Services, Administration for Children and Families, Administration on Children, Youth and Families, Children's Bureau, 2013. Child Maltreatment 2012. Available from http://www.acf.hhs.gov/programs/cb/research-data-technology/statistics-research/child-maltreatment.

Investigation and Evidence Collection

4

The Multidisciplinary Team Approach and Child Advocacy Center Model

Child advocacy centers provide a neutral, safe, child-friendly environment, which is most conducive to children's disclosure. Child advocacy centers typically have trained forensic interviewers on staff to conduct the interview one-on-one in a private interview room that is set up to suit the child's needs. The investigative team members assigned to the case should be present to observe the interview from an observation room as it takes place, as well as participate in the pre- and post-forensic interview discussion, which provides them with the opportunity to communicate on a higher level with one another and with the non-offending caregiver (NOC) of the child. Case management, protective factors, and investigative measures, such as the need for a medical examination and referrals for therapeutic intervention are discussed among the investigative team members during this process, which results in shared decision making in the investigation.

The National Children's Alliance (NCA) offers accreditation for child advocacy centers. Services provided by child advocacy centers that are required by the NCA to meet standards for accreditation include forensic interviewing (conducted by interviewers who are trained in and practice a nationally recognized model), family advocacy, medical and mental health services, case tracking, and case review. Child advocacy centers are also required to practice cultural competency, the multidisciplinary team (MDT) approach, and they must have organization capacity, such as nonprofit status, or be a part of a governmental entity.

Case review is an important component of the child advocacy center model. In order to meet accreditation standards for practice, child advocacy centers must organize case review on a regular basis in each county served. Case review brings each of the core investigative disciplines together to discuss case status and outcomes. These disciplines include law enforcement, child protective services (CPS), juvenile justice, medical, mental health, prosecution, and child advocacy center personnel. The purpose of case review is to provide increased communication and shared

Child Abuse Investigation Field Guide.
Copyright © 2015 Elsevier Inc. All rights reserved.

decision making among the agencies that get involved in the investigation of child abuse.

By utilizing the MDT approach in addition to the services of a child advocacy center, the focus of the investigation is child centered. In other words, decisions throughout the criminal justice process are made by the agencies involved working in collaboration putting the child's needs first along the way.

Some communities do not have access to child advocacy center services due to lack of resources or organizational capacity. It is highly recommended; regardless of whether there is access to a center, every community should exercise the MDT approach when handling these sensitive cases. Ideally, the MDT will have designated members from each of the core disciplines that become involved in the investigation of child abuse: law enforcement, CPS, juvenile justice, prosecution, mental health, and medical services, who work together on these cases. Written protocol incorporating the practices of each discipline should be created with the input of all agencies, which serves as a living document to provide guidance for collaboration and investigative best practices.

First Responders

When an allegation of child abuse occurs and there is an indication that a crime has been committed against a child, if the alleged abuse occurs within the home or is at the hands of a caregiver of the child, a coinvestigation between law enforcement and CPS must ensue. It is best if, once the report is received by either agency, it is cross-reported to the other to ensure that both parties begin to collaborate from the beginning of the investigation. CPS and law enforcement should run background checks in their databases on the family and the alleged perpetrator to gain as much knowledge as possible regarding related priors when initiating their investigation.

It is recommended that each agency assign investigators who are trained together in MDT best practice in response to criminal investigations of child abuse. Although each discipline has a specific purpose in their role, decision making during the investigative process should go hand-in-hand. This is a joint process. When CPS and law enforcement work together to determine whether or not abuse occurs, this minimizes trauma to the child and family, avoids duplication of efforts, and makes the investigative process more efficient and reliable.

Investigative Interviews

The goal of investigative interviews is to elicit reliable information during the course of an investigation. In addition to MDT training, it is critical that investigators receive specialized training in interviewing victims, witnesses, and suspects. In short, interviews must be conducted in a respectful, nonjudgmental manner. Open-ended questioning by investigators will elicit narrative responses, and the depth and breadth of information will be much more detailed and reliable. Investigators should avoid asking leading questions, in an effort to remove their personal bias from the interview. Careful consideration should be given to entertaining alternative explanations for the abuse throughout the investigation to avoid assumptions being made which could result in faulty conclusions.

When conducting interviews, professionals must keep in mind that people are affected by numerous physical and emotional factors that can color or destroy the validity of the information they give to investigators. Emotions may cause a person to give prejudicial information, to lie, or to forget events. Lighting, distance, or other physical limitations may result in an inaccurate interpretation of the event observed. Studies indicate that individuals who are placed in traumatic circumstances tend to not be able to recall details or events accurately. The interview setting can have a dramatic impact on the information gained from the interviewee as well. The least chaotic environment, free from distractions or the influence of other witnesses, is most conducive to gathering clear, accurate information.

The officer or CPS worker seeking to arrive at the truth must evaluate carefully the information obtained from all interviews, piecing the information together to create a picture of the dynamics of the situation and the possible incident(s) of abuse. He or she must recognize individual differences and limitations and be aware of the personal motives that may be involved. They must also possess the necessary skills to persuade the obstinate to cooperate, and potentially exert authority to ensure cooperation when necessary.

Types of Investigative Interviews

Interview (Hess, 1997)

This is a conversation with the purpose of obtaining and evaluating information given to law enforcement officers and CPS investigators by persons who have knowledge of the events or circumstances of a crime, accident, or other matter of police interest.

Interrogation

This is the process of asking questions of a person arrested or suspected of a crime and is utilized by law enforcement during the course of their investigation. It is generally considered an interrogation when the questions that are asked could incriminate the individual if answered. When the interview changes to interrogation Miranda must be considered. This line of questioning should be limited to suspects and avoided when interviewing other types of witnesses. Typically CPS workers do not participate in this line of questioning.

Field Interviews

These are street-level encounters or contacts with individuals initiated by law enforcement officers in an effort to obtain information relating to an investigation into criminal activity, specific complaint or other matter of "police interest." This may include the need to briefly interview the child victim in an effort to determine if there is cause to initiate an investigation or determine safety needs. When it is deemed necessary to do so with a child victim in the investigation of child abuse, CPS or law enforcement will conduct a "cursory" or "minimal facts" interview. This interview should be conducted by a professional who is trained in child abuse forensic interviewing, but modified to collect minimal data to assess safety or initiate the investigation (see the Minimal Facts Interview section (p. 73)). A detailed child forensic interview should not be conducted in the field, but rather in a child advocacy center or child-friendly, neutral, safe setting (see the Forensic Interview section (p. 72)).

Statement

Definition: A single declaration, remark, or assertion; a report of facts or opinions; the act or process of stating or presenting orally or on paper. A voluntary statement form is often given to an interviewee so that the police officer may obtain written information in the victim's/witness's own words. It is frequently used as an addition to the oral interview.

Witness Interview Considerations

When interviewing each type of witness as defined in the next section (i.e., reporter, outcry witness, NOC, corroborative witnesses, child/victim/sibling, and suspects), the following standard concepts and procedures should be considered (Reid and Associates, 2008).

Status (Emotions and Attitudes)

1. What is the person's (victim, witness, or suspect) physical condition?
2. Investigators must be able to evaluate information provided by persons who are emotionally charged during an incident. This information, coupled with facts, should be taken into consideration while attempting to verify the reliability and credibility of a witness.

Personal Data

1. Consider that age may play a role in how the person perceives the incident—elderly and very young will require special consideration. With this in mind, consider that all children should be interviewed by a trained forensic interviewer.
2. Race, sex, and ethnic group will also affect how a person perceives an event.
3. Cultural bias and practices may influence what the person believes happened.
4. Education may also play a role in how the person describes the event.

Emotional State

1. The victim and witness may well have different emotional and physical states (e.g., the victim may be in shock and the witness may appear more upset than the victim for having seen the incident).
2. The suspect may display any range of emotions and attitudes (e.g., tearful, angry, fearful, nervous, or calm). Don't be fooled by these reactions.

Attitude

1. Cooperative—usually the easiest to deal with, but be careful with someone who is *too* eager. Ask yourself what the person stands to gain for providing this information.
2. Reluctant—not unusual, find out why:
   a. Don't have time to get involved.
   b. Afraid of retaliation.
   c. Don't like police.
   d. Bad previous experience.
   e. Peer pressure.
3. Hostile—why? (background information can be very helpful and important in determining this).
   a. Be alert, hostile people can become aggressive people.
   b. If possible, have backup.

Interviewer Considerations

1. Don'ts:
   a. Don't pre-judge.
   b. Don't let prejudice or biases show.
   c. Don't show anger.
   d. Don't be sarcastic.
2. Do's:
   a. Be pleasant, polite, and interested in what the interviewee is saying.
   b. Keep the parties informed. Explain what will happen next and let him or her know why you are asking certain questions.
   c. Detain for as little time as possible; cooperation is a two-way street!
   d. Get the facts, ask the questions without emotions.

Communication Skills of Interviewee

How well the interviewee is able to verbalize is one of the most important variables in interviewing, as is how well he or she understands the interviewer's questions. Level of education, physical and mental condition, and emotional state all enter into the picture. Adults with developmental disabilities should be interviewed in the same manner as a child victim or witness. Make sure that a trained forensic interviewer conducts these interviews in a safe, neutral, setting, sensitive to the interviewee's needs. If there is access to child advocacy center services in your community, most centers will interview adults with disabilities at the request of the investigative team. Check your local child advocacy center protocol to inquire if this service is available to you.

Communication Skills of Interviewer

The interviewer must be able to make himself or herself understood by the interviewee (normally, simple questions are best). Communicating on the interviewee's level is important. Most important are the interviewer's listening skills. Listen intently. Listen with your ears *and* your eyes. Listen to voice pitch and inflection. Listen for contradictions. Listen for what is not said, as well as what is said. Body language, while not an exact science, can give insight into the validity and truthfulness of information.

Interview Environment

The location of the interview cannot always be controlled by the investigators in the field. Safety is an important factor for both investigators and interviewee, but other factors should be taken into consideration in order for the interview to produce a successful outcome. Try to secure a place where the interviewee can be afforded privacy. Ideally, there should be no external distractions such as telephones or other background noises. As long as safety is not compromised, one investigator (CPS or law enforcement) can conduct an interview with the other sitting nearby. When this technique is employed, one should assume the role of "note taker/observer" while the other does the speaking.

Investigators should consider removing physical barriers such as tables and plants. The presence of these items seems unassuming; however, depending on their location they can serve as a "psychological wall" between the officer and interviewee.

Interviewer's Behavior

Investigators should be acutely aware of the behavior of an interviewee. However, they must realize that the person is observing his or her behavior as well. Your body language is equally important. When interviewing witnesses, sit at their level to put them at ease. When engaging children, it is preferable that weapons are not visible. Officers might consider keeping a lightweight jacket on hand to put on in the event they must conduct a field interview of a child during the initial response.

Types of Questions (Funnel Approach)

When considering the manner in which a witness interview should begin, it is recommended to ask open-ended questions. These questions require explanation and tend to produce a great deal of information from the witness up front. This approach invites interviewees to speak in their own words and encourage full answers. Use the interviewee's words and terminology when asking subsequent questions. Once investigators have a general idea of "what happened" they can narrow responses by honing in on details and probing for more information. "Close-ended" (multiple choice or yes/no questions) are necessary for clarification, but should be used sparingly. Asking closed-ended questions consecutively would be considered suggestible since it may result in forced choice responses. When asking a closed-ended, or "focused" question, interviewers should follow it up with an open-ended question, offering the interviewee the opportunity to expand on his or her previous response (American Professional Society on the Abuse of Children, 2012).

Interview Timing

As a general rule, the most appropriate time to conduct an interview is as soon as possible after an incident. Individual circumstances may prevent this from happening and any number of factors may influence the investigator's ability to conduct the interview in a timely manner. For example, the victim may be emotionally distraught or physically injured and his or her medical needs may take precedence over conducting the initial interview, or a witness may be difficult to locate. Nevertheless, the general rule is the sooner the interview takes place, the better the information provided will be. Delays in interviewing witnesses and victims can result in influences that can change statements or even cause recantation.

Case Background Information

Investigators should gather as much information possible about the incident or events before beginning interviews. In some cases, officers may know only what the dispatcher passes on to them, or CPS workers may know only what was shared by the reporter. When at all possible, take the time to prepare more adequately prior to interviewing. The parties and agencies listed below are only some of the sources of background information that may be helpful in this process.

Resources

1. CPS/Law Enforcement Databases

You may have information already on file at your own department; you will not know unless you inquire. Check all persons and property through National Crime Information Center (NCIC) as well as local "in-house" sources. A neighboring jurisdiction may be working a case on the person you are now investigating. Officers should always attempt to develop good working relationships with local, state, and federal officials.

2. Medical Doctors/Personnel

Doctors do not necessarily have to answer your questions, especially if they are medical questions; however, HIPAA (Health Insurance Portability and Accountability Act) regulations (which are Federal) do not apply in child abuse cases. Section 160.203 sets forth a series of exceptions to general HIPAA privacy requirements. It also clarifies that HIPAA generally overrides state laws where they are contrary to HIPAA. Because of ethical concerns, many doctors may not want to talk to you, although you will never know unless you ask. All states have laws that mandate reporting of suspected child abuse or neglect, and HIPAA rules allow disclosure of protected health information without legal guardian authorization under these circumstances. In general, if a pediatrician suspects abuse or neglect, as defined within state statutes, then he or she is obligated to disclose information to the appropriate investigative agencies, which in most states includes CPS and law enforcement agencies.

If you cannot get badly needed information by asking, then the doctor may be served with a subpoena. Discuss this with your solicitor if you think it is necessary. Be sure the information is vital to the case before you take such drastic measures.

3. Department of Juvenile Justice

The DJJ may have valuable information in cases involving juvenile offenders. Most jurisdictions coinvestigate these crimes utilizing the MDT approach, just as they would crimes involving adult suspects. Check your state statute and local policies and procedures to inquire how this will work in your community.

4. Department of Probation, Pardon, and Parole

Making contact with a suspect's probation officer could provide valuable information as to the former's criminal history. There could also be active warrants against the individual.

5. School Officials/Teachers/Counselors

Although hesitant to incriminate students for offenses outside the school, these people can offer a great deal of information that can be helpful to investigators in making their determination of abuse or neglect.

6. Ministers/Church Personnel

As with school officials, church personnel will probably not reveal anything of an incriminating nature about a member, but can help if the case is related to church in some way. Be aware of the priest/minister privilege.

Documentation

Notes

Take notes, not only on the information you obtain, but on your observations as well. If the subject has identification details, write down what type and the number as well as the complete name, address, and date of birth. This information could turn out to be important later. Many police departments have created field interview forms, which serve as a formal means of tracking the interactions between law enforcement and the person, particularly when there is no arrest involved.

Taking Statements

When the term "statement" is used, it normally implies a more formal and structured interview. Oftentimes it becomes necessary for an officer to take a statement at the scene of a call for service. For example, an officer investigating a call of domestic violence may be better served by obtaining a statement from the victim while still at the scene. In most cases when a statement is required a serious crime, accident, or event has occurred. It may be necessary to take statements from persons in a more formal setting such as the police department or other environment. This is especially true if the statement is being taken from a suspect.

Methods of taking statements (Walters and Associates, 2010):

1. Verbal

A verbal statement (only) from a subject is better than nothing, but it is very easily recanted later. Never discourage a verbal statement, but always try to take it one step further to written form. If this proves unsuccessful, try to have another witness present while taking the verbal statement.

2. Written

If the subject is literate, allow him or her to write the entire statement in his or her own words. If there is still need for further clarification at the end, add any questions you need to ask and the answers given by the subject. If the subject is unable to write the statement it is acceptable for an officer to write it for him or her. Ensure that the statement is transcribed exactly as the individual dictates it to you (verbatim). Do not paraphrase or add your own words or interpretations. Always have the subject sign and date the statement and have the signing witnessed by a third party. A copy of the signed statement should be provided to the subject. Ensure that it includes the fact that "I have read the statement, it is true and accurate to the best of my knowledge" and that he or she has "received a copy."

3. Recorded

A recorded statement usually carries more weight in court because it not only presents the story in the subject's own words, but allows the listener/viewer to detect emotions and moods. It can also reassure the listener or viewer that the statement was not forced or coerced and that no one "put words in the subject's mouth." When recording a statement by audio or video, always begin by giving the date, time, location, list of persons present, and topic of the statement (interview). Inform the subject that you are recording so he or she cannot later claim that he or she did not know. Once the interview begins, do not turn the recorder off until the interview is complete. To turn it off and on during the interview may cause a listener to suspect that the tape has been edited or that while the tape was off the subject was being rehearsed or threatened. Remember that background noise and conversations will be picked up on the tape so take care in selecting your location. A quiet, distraction-free area is essential.

Order of Progression (Initial Interview)

Listed below is a suggested order and progression of a typical witness interview (Hess, 1997):

1. Identify self.
2. Create favorable atmosphere and build rapport.
3. Interviewee's free narrative—encourage interviewee to talk; do not interrupt.
4. Question and answer—get specific information; "pin down" and resolve inconsistencies.
5. Get all the facts.
6. Use comparisons.
7. Separate fact from inference.
8. Verify and test.
9. Summarize and obtain descriptions where appropriate.
10. Close.

Types of Witnesses

Oftentimes it is difficult to determine initially who is a suspect and who is a witness and if there is even any difference. Law enforcement and CPS workers must obtain information and figure out what happened and what is truthful. This will require talking to various people involved (Walters and Associates, 2010).

Reporter

The reporter should be the first person the investigator contacts at the onset of the investigation. This interview will assist the investigator in determining if the reporter has a bias and is a reliable source. It may also be helpful in determining whether the child victim is currently at risk, whether the NOC is supportive of the child, and whether the alleged perpetrator currently has access to the child or family.

Outcry Witness

From the interview of the outcry witness, investigators can gather information to determine the circumstances of the child's initial disclosure. This should also occur early on in the investigation. Oftentimes, the outcry witness and the reporter are one and the same. Knowing whether the disclosure was given upon questioning or given spontaneously, can help investigators assess from the beginning if biases or misinterpretations regarding the child's initial statement exist. It is important to learn from the outcry witness: Who was present during the child's initial disclosure? What were the circumstances of the disclosure? What was the reaction of the outcry witness to the child's statement? What was the child's emotional state during the disclosure? And what were the next immediate steps that were taken by the outcry witness once he or she received the information? Investigators may also be able to glean whether the NOC is supportive or protective of the child.

Non-Offending Caregiver

The interview of the NOC can prove to be critical in the investigation of child abuse. This should occur early on in the investigation, typically occurring as the next step after speaking with the reporter, unless the reporter indicates otherwise or there is other evidence that the NOC is not supportive or protective of the child; then, of course, making contact with the child to assess safety is paramount. Investigators must be familiar with their state statutes related to making contact with children with or without parental consent (see Resources section (p. 65)).

In an effort to determine whether the NOC is cooperative, investigators should take care in establishing rapport with him or her at the initial stage of the investigation. In doing so, it is helpful for investigators to be familiar with research that explains how NOCs experience the criminal justice process and how they react to learning of the allegations of abuse of their child.

Research and national statistical data over the past several years have shown that in most cases of abuse (95% across studies), the child knows their offender. This would indicate that the NOC knows the offender as well. When abuse occurs within the home, it is often assumed that the NOC was just as culpable as the offender as they must have known about the abuse but did not stop it. However, research shows that the majority of non-offending parents do not realize their child is being victimized. In most cases, the NOC (usually the mother), does believe, support, and is willing to protect their child. Investigators must consider when a parent does not realize the abuse is occurring, especially when the abuse is within the family or at the hands of the parent's significant other; it is normal for the parent's initial reaction to be that of shock, disbelief, and even denial. This reaction is not a clear predictor for the parent's protective capacities. With support and increased communication from professionals involved in their case, even ambivalent NOCs will protect their child. With this knowledge, investigators must be prepared to reach out to the NOC using a supportive, unbiased approach, to assist the parent in supporting their child during the investigation and court process.

Additionally, research indicates that support from a loving caregiver can significantly lessen the experience of trauma by the child. Investigators must also realize that many caregivers may have been abused themselves as children and, thus, may react strongly to their child's disclosure of child abuse. Being sensitive to the parent's needs as well as the child's is critical to the investigation and their cooperation throughout the criminal justice process. Therapeutic services for both the child and caregivers is an important step in the process and should be offered as soon as there is an indication that abuse occurred.

There are also cases in which NOCs do not support or protect their child. Investigators must keep a watchful eye on the relationship between the NOC and the child so that corrective action can be taken if the relationship is observed to be unsupportive, or the NOC has demonstrated their allegiance to the offender, which can be detrimental to the child and lead to recantation. In these instances, protective custody or reliable kinship placement would be the suggested course of action until the NOC's perception and actions can be rehabilitated (Walters, S. (2002), Working with the non-offending caregiver. Sex Offender Law Report, 4(3), 35–38).

Eyewitness

An eyewitness is someone who has seen part or all of the incident. Just as different people have different skills, strengths, and weaknesses, eyewitness accounts may vary greatly from one eyewitness to another. Studies have shown that on average, eyewitness accounts may only be about 50% accurate. In fact, the Innocence Project has shown that eyewitness misidentification is the single greatest cause of wrongful convictions nationwide, playing a role in 72% of convictions overturned through DNA testing. While eyewitness testimony can be persuasive evidence before a judge or jury, 30 years of strong social science research has proven that eyewitness identification is often unreliable (Innocence Project). There are many reasons for this. One is that our minds do not work like a video recorder; we cannot just play things back as they actually happened but we play them back the way we have filed them in our memories. Seeing an event from a different angle than someone else, like replays on the football field, will give the eyewitness a different perspective. This does not mean that their statements have no value. They may be able to help add information to the investigation that helps law enforcement and the CPS worker put all the pieces together.

Investigators should keep in mind that in cases of child sexual abuse, there will rarely be an eyewitness. If there is, the witness could likely be traumatized by witnessing the event, and, therefore, special care and sensitivity should be given during the course of the interview. If the eyewitness is a child, the child should be interviewed forensically, utilizing the same practices that would be taken when interviewing child victims.

Corroborative Witnesses

Corroborative witnesses can provide information that will assist in verifying that something happened or did not happen. Once the reporter, outcry witness, NOC, and the child are interviewed, investigators should interview corroborative witnesses who may be able to confirm or refute facts revealed in their statements. Corroborative witnesses can include, but are not limited to, family members, friends, school personnel, medical and mental health professionals, and even the suspect. Oftentimes, even if there is not a confession to the crime, the suspect will corroborate non-abuse facts shared by the child or other witnesses that will show proof of the child's credibility and could be seen as a partial confession. Corroborative witness interviews are key, especially in cases of child sexual abuse, when there is rarely physical evidence, and much of the credibility of the case rests on the statements provided by all the witnesses involved.

Child Victim/Witness/Sibling Interviews

Forensic Interview

The forensic interview is often the foundation of the investigation. The purpose of the forensic interview is to obtain factual, investigative information in an effort to determine whether or not abuse occurred. The forensic interview may reveal critical evidence, and other potential victims or witnesses to be interviewed, as well as the dynamics of the abuse the child has experienced. Forensic interviewers are trained to gather information from the child in a way that is sensitive to his or her needs and cognitive development. The depth and breadth of a forensic interview can be extensive, including contextual details of the event, exploring alternative explanations, looking at source monitoring, and more advanced issues in collecting data. Forensic interviews go beyond determining "Who, What, When, and Where," by inquiring "How" the abuse occurred, in an effort to assess the child's overall experience and gather as much corroborative detail as possible for the purposes of the investigation.

It is critical that the forensic interview is conducted competently by a professional who has attended, and practices research-based techniques learned in, a 5-day nationally recognized forensic interview course such as those offered through the following reputable national organizations: American Professional Society on the Abuse of Children, CornerHouse, Gunderson National Child Protection Training Center, National Children's Advocacy Center, and National Institute of Child Heath and Human Development.

As stated earlier, it is recommended that the child forensic interview be conducted at a child advocacy center. This provides a neutral, safe, child-friendly environment, which is most conducive to children's disclosure. Many communities do not have access to child advocacy center services. In those cases, it is important that the community stakeholders of the core investigative agencies develop and take part in the MDT approach. In the absence of a child-friendly interview facility, the forensic interview should be conducted by an investigator trained in a nationally recognized forensic interview model, and it should take place one-on-one, in the most comfortable environment for the child, with no distractions. It is best if the interview can be digitally recorded on video, but at the very least, an audio recording should be made to capture the manner in which the child was questioned, and the child's responses.

For the purposes of this field guide, offering a "how to" guide to forensic interviewing would be too in-depth. Again, it must be emphasized that professionals who are charged with the responsibility of conducting forensic interviews of children should attend one of the nationally recognized forensic interview trainings offered through the organizations listed above. Web sites for those organizations with additional information regarding forensic interview training are provided in the Resources section of this guide.

Minimal Facts Interview

The purpose of the minimal facts interview is to elicit reliable information in order to begin the investigative process. There are some cases in which the child makes no, or limited disclosure to the outcry witness. In order to initiate the report of a crime, and in some situations, determine whether the child is safe and protected, it might be necessary for a minimal facts interview to be conducted prior to the forensic interview.

It should be noted that if investigators are able to gather information needed from the reporter, the outcry witness, or the NOC to initiate a report or assess safety of a child, then it would not be necessary to conduct a minimal facts interview. Instead the child should be referred directly for a forensic interview, bypassing the minimal facts interview altogether. This minimizes the number of times children are required to go through the interview process, thus minimizing trauma to the child.

If there is a need for the minimal facts interview, the interview should be conducted by a professional who has had training in forensic interviewing of children. This will ensure the interviewer practices research-based techniques sensitive to the child's needs, and has a basic knowledge of child development, linguistics, and the process of disclosure and dynamics of abuse. In addition to having been trained in forensic interviewing, the interviewer should feel comfortable communicating with children, and comfortable discussing the topic of concern.

The interviewer should avoid leading questions and not make assumptions. It is critical that investigators set aside their personal bias, which can be rooted in their past experience or work with the family, and come into the case with a completely open mind. The interviewer should not be focused solely on the allegation at hand, but, rather, be open to other explanations, or other types of abuse that may be occurring to the child or in their home.

Background information that could be gathered from a supportive NOC prior to the minimal facts interview, and that might be helpful to the interviewer, includes the child's developmental level, cultural considerations, medical or psychological impairments, family composition, prior disclosures, the child's understanding of the nature of the allegations, behavioral changes in the child related to their disclosure or the timeline of abuse, any other possible witnesses to the abuse, a history of domestic violence in the home, possible misunderstanding of the allegations, and possible motivation for false allegations being made.

When conducting the minimal facts interview, the setting is the key. The responding investigator(s) should select the location most comfortable to the child, one that is safe, with no distractions, and preferably neutral. This interview should be conducted one-on-one, and digitally recorded, preferably on video, but at the very least on audio. The child should be made aware of the means of documentation. If two investigators are present, it should be determined ahead of time who is most qualified to interview the child. If it is not possible to digitally record the interview, the investigator not conducting the interview should sit quietly to the side and take detailed notes, written verbatim, with quotes, and describe the child's emotions as well.

The interview should take place without the presence of parents, caregivers, other children, school personnel, or other professionals, giving the child as much privacy as possible, and reducing the number of potential witnesses. The interview should not take place if the alleged perpetrator is on the premises.

These minimal facts interview guidelines were developed based on the basic tenets of forensic interviewing. Again, the information in this section does not replace the necessity for forensic interview training, but is being provided in this guide for professionals in support of their efforts where there is a need to conduct a minimal facts interview as part of the criminal investigation.

This process incorporates three stages, which should be present in each interview (see below). The difference between a minimal facts interview and a forensic interview is brevity. The forensic interview will include the gathering of explicit details and as much information as possible about the topic of concern, whereas the minimal facts interview will only gather enough information to assess safety or establish that a potential crime occurred.

The minimal facts interview stages: (1) introductory, (2) information gathering, and (3) closure. The interviewer should be flexible when interviewing the child. For example, if the child immediately discloses as soon as the interview begins, it would be most appropriate not to interrupt the child, but to continue through the information gathering stage, and then later go back for background information acquired in the introductory stage, if needed. Always bring the interview to an end with the closure stage only.

1. *Introductory stage*: It is important at the onset of the interview that the child is oriented to the purpose and provided with an appropriate explanation of the interview process and guidelines, or ground rules, for the interview. This is also where rapport building begins, establishing a dialogue with the child, encouraging them to talk about things that are important and familiar to them (including family). This is also a time when the interviewer will begin to assess the child's willingness and ability to speak in narrative form.

   Rapport building should continue throughout the interview, with the interviewer maintaining a neutral, nonjudgmental stance, expressing little emotional response to the child's disclosure, while showing compassion and empathy.

   When orienting the child to the purpose of the interview, the interviewer should briefly introduce him- or herself to the child and explain that part of their job is to talk with kids about different things that are going on in the kids' lives. If there is another investigator present during the interview (either observing in the room or from another location), they should be acknowledged as well, and the child should be made aware of their reason for being there. The interviewer should be upfront about their means for documentation. If the child's words are being recorded, he or she should be made aware of this. The interviewer should explain why they are being recorded, and a simple way to do so is by saying that the recording will help the interviewer remember what was said.

   When initiating building rapport, the interviewer should engage the child by discussing topics that are interesting and familiar to the youngster (e.g., ask about the child's favorite things to do, ask about school and daily activities).

   Example: "Let me know a little bit about you. What do you like to do for fun?"

   This allows the interviewer to assess the child's willingness/ability to speak in narrative, and it allows the child the opportunity to engage in a dialogue with the interviewer about something that interests the child, of which the child is the expert. This is also a time when the interviewer can ask who the child lives with, in an effort to determine the child's perspective of their family.

   Once the child is aware of the purpose of the interview and rapport building has begun, these four issues, or "ground rules," should always be discussed:

   - If the interviewer makes a mistake, it is important for the child to correct the interviewer and fix the mistake.
   - It is important that the child does not guess about anything, and if they do not know the answer, it is OK to let the interviewer know this.

- If the child does not understand the interviewer, it is important to let the interviewer know, and the question will be asked in a different way.
- It is important for the child to tell the truth, and only talk about what is real.

2. *Information gathering stage*: the purpose of this stage is to gather factual information about the alleged abuse determining:
   Who—including the alleged perpetrator and other potential witnesses/victims.
   What—in very simple terms, no need for extensive detail if the forensic interview is to be scheduled.
   When—focus on the last incident to determine the need for an acute medical examination or evidence collection.
   Where—determine jurisdiction; if abuse occurred in more than one location, establish each one, if possible, so that the appropriate law enforcement agencies can be notified and participate in the MDT approach and the forensic interview process.

Initiating Disclosure

When transitioning from the introductory stage to information gathering, ask, "Do you know why I am here to talk with you today?" types of questions. Hopefully, the child will begin disclosure at that point. If not, use the "funnel" approach, which becomes progressively more focused in an effort to obtain information needed to move forward.

Funnel Approach

Examples of the "funnel approach" will follow this fact pattern: A 7-year-old female disclosed to her mother that her grandfather touched her pee pee and it hurt. To initiate disclosure, the interviewer should start with a broad question, and if there is no disclosure, become more direct, providing prompts based on facts provided by the outcry witness (in this case her mother), to determine jurisdiction and when the last incident occurred (if her mother cannot provide that information).

Interviewer: "Do you know why you came here to talk with me today?"

If no disclosure, become more direct:

Interviewer: "I understand you came here today to tell me about something that happened to you."

If no disclosure, become more direct:

Interviewer: "I understand you talked with someone about something that happened to you."

If no disclosure, become more direct. With the outcry witness's permission, reference the child's previous disclosure.

Interviewer: "I understand you told your mom that someone did something to you."

If no disclosure, become more direct. Introducing the allegation without mentioning the alleged perpetrator may be necessary under emergency circumstances when safety is of concern:

Interviewer: "I understand you told your mom that someone touched you in a way you didn't like."

If no disclosure, become more direct:

Interviewer: "I understand you told your mom someone touched your pee pee and it hurt."

If still no disclosure, allow the child to acknowledge something occurred that they do not want to talk about with you:

Interviewer: "Did something happen to you that you don't want to talk about with me today?"

At this point, with no disclosure, it would be inappropriate to go further in the information gathering stage. The interviewer should move toward the closure stage and ask safety questions. See Closure stage.

Open-Ended Questions

If the child does initiate disclosure, follow up with open-ended questions to elicit the information needed (remember, limited to Who, What, When, Where, *not* How). It is important to quickly determine if there were multiple incidents. Once the child discloses something happened, determine if it occurred "one time or more than one time." Do not ask "How many times" as this may elicit inaccurate information, or the child may guess. Follow the line of questioning as suggested below:

Who/what question:

Interviewer: "What happened?"

Child: "Grandpa touched me."

When question:

Interviewer: "Did grandpa touch you one time, or more than one time?"

Child: "More than one time."

Interviewer: "Tell me about the last time."
Child: "It was during Christmas break when I was in the second grade."
What question:
Interviewer: "What part of your body did grandpa touch?"
Child: "My pee pee."
Where question:
Interviewer: "Where were you when grandpa touched your pee pee during Christmas break?"
Child: "In the basement of his house."
Where question (additional jurisdiction):
Interviewer: "Did this happen at any other place?"
Child: "At my house."
Where question:
Interviewer: "Did it happen somewhere else?"
Child: "No."

If the interviewer is able to obtain this much information, this should be sufficient to create an incident report and refer the child for a forensic interview to take place at a child advocacy center or a safe, child-friendly, neutral location. If every jurisdiction is identified, this allows the investigators to ensure law enforcement from each jurisdiction is notified and can be present to observe the forensic interview when it takes place.

If the incident occurred recently, and there is a possibility that evidence might be present, there may be further need for additional questioning to obtain a search warrant in the event law enforcement is unable to gain "consent to search."

Additional Questions (Witness Related)

- Ask the child if someone else knows what happened.
- Ask the child if someone else saw what happened.

Safety Questions

- Ask the child if they have seen the alleged perpetrator since this happened.
- Ask the child if they were to see or hear from the alleged perpetrator, who could they tell?
- Ask the child how their mom/dad/family reacted when learning about what happened.
- Ask the child what has happened since they told.
- Ask the child if they are worried about anything right now.
- Ask the child if they feel safe.

Additional Interviewing Tips

- Although this is a "minimal facts" interview, the child may provide more detail than needed. Allow them to talk. Do not shut them down.
- Be patient. Let the child set the pace for the interview.
- Soften your tone.
- Use the child's language.
- Ask developmentally appropriate questions. If a child is unable to provide information due to their cognitive abilities, we can oftentimes rely on adults or corroborative witnesses to help fill in the blanks. As a rule, preschool age children (5 years and younger) are unable to understand abstract concepts. Therefore, they will likely be unable to provide time frames or information about who else may know about what happened. Investigators should avoid questions beyond the child's developmental level, as this will likely result in inaccurate information.
- Every case and every child is different. Be open to all explanations for concerns that are reported.
- Do not pressure a reluctant or frustrated child. This compromises the investigation and the child's credibility. It may result in the child minimizing the abuse or denying that the abuse occurred.
- Do not use seductive/coaxing techniques in an effort to get the child to cooperate. Example: "If you tell me what happened, I will let you pick out a stuffed animal."
- Give the child a sense of control in the interview. Follow their lead in the interview and tie your questions to facts they have already revealed (see examples provided in "funnel approach.")
- If you do ask a direct question (yes/no or multiple choice), follow it up with an open-ended question to allow the child to expand on their response.
- If you ask a multiple choice question, leave the third option open for the child to fill in the blank (e.g., "Were you in the bedroom, the bathroom, or somewhere else?").
- Do not paraphrase and ask the child to confirm what was said. Instead, repeat their statements back to them one at a time and pause for confirmation or correction from the child.
- Do not challenge the child on inconsistencies in the interview, instead, *clarify*. If the child states something that is inconsistent with information they already provided, let the child know you do not understand in this way, "I'm confused, I think you said ___ before, help me understand what you mean."
- Do not challenge what doesn't make sense. Ask, "What makes you remember it that way?"
- Don't make promises. No one can guarantee what will happen once the child leaves the interview room. We cannot guarantee safety, or that it will not happen to them again.

- Don't tell the child that the alleged perpetrator will go to jail. This may not be the outcome the child is looking for, and again, there are no guarantees.
- *Remember* Listen more and talk less.

3. *Closure stage*: The purpose of the closure stage is to bring a respectful end to the interview. When transitioning from information gathering to closure, simply ask the child if they have questions about what was discussed. Then make certain to cover these points:
   - Explain that a forensic interview will take place, and, if the information is available, when and where this will occur.
   - Ask the child to identify trusted people they can turn to if they were to need help in the future. Don't relate this to abuse, keep it general.
   - End the interview on a topic that is not related to the abuse, such as asking what their plans are for the rest of the day, if that is appropriate.
   - Thank the child for taking time to speak with you.

Suspect Interview

A suspect usually possesses the most significant information since he or she was also a "witness" to the incident. A suspect can also supply insight as to the motive. Investigators should gather as much intelligence as possible about the suspect prior to the interview. In cases involving allegations of child sexual abuse, the child should be interviewed forensically, as well as corroborative parties and eyewitnesses before interviewing the suspect. In emergency situations this could pose a challenge for patrol officers, as this information is typically gathered from many sources.

Although most patrol officers will not be Mirandizing suspects as often as departmental investigators, all officers should be familiar with the basic premise of the Miranda warning. If the suspect is in custody (not free to leave) AND the officer intends to ask the suspect questions that may elicit an incriminating response, the suspect should be Mirandized prior to questioning. Although the typical "street encounter" or "field interview" does not require that an individual be advised of his or her rights prior to engaging in conversation with law enforcement, the latter agency must be careful to consider whether both conditions of Miranda have been met. The standard of "reasonableness" applies to all interactions with officers. Reasonableness will vary depending on the situation and context of the encounter. Officers should know their jurisdictions policy and adhere to that.

It is estimated that 80% of human communication is nonverbal (Walters and Associates, 2010). Lying takes skill and practice as does the police interview. It is difficult for the brain and the body not to be in concert with each other. If the spoken word is inconsistent with the body language at the time of the response or immediately thereafter then this should be of great concern to the interviewer. A *physiological response* is the unconscious and involuntary response that people say or show when they are under stress; the response can be verbal or nonverbal (Joseph, 1995). There are several outward behaviors that the interviewer can watch for to help evaluate information garnered from interviews. Typically they occur in clusters; that is, more than one may be presented at the same time. They include:

1. Loss of eye contact
2. Adjusting clothes/jewelry
3. Crossing of the legs
4. Gazing into the distance
5. Rubbing the hands, back of the head or neck
6. Sweating or scratching
7. Laughing/smiling.

These nonverbal indicators are useless, however, without the interviewer establishing baseline characteristics for the individual (Joseph, 1995). Interviews should begin with basic information such as name and address in order for the officer to observe the response and begin to establish a rapport. This helps the interviewer to become familiar with the "normal" behavior of the interviewee. Once the "norm" has been established, officers can delve further for specific information and observe his or her response to more challenging questions. This process assists in evaluating the reliability, believability, and accuracy of information provided by the interviewee.

There are both verbal and nonverbal physiological responses the interviewer should be on the lookout for to determine "normal" behavior patterns. Verbal responses such as a period of silence before the answer (which may be masked by a cough or other sound), the repetition of the question the interviewer just asked the interviewee, or complaining of various issues (high blood pressure, temperature of room/conditions) may be indications of deception. Nonverbal cues such as tapping, stuttering, crying, showing remorse, wringing of hands, or evasive positions (turning chair away, hiding face) should also be observed closely to determine whether these responses should be considered normal behavior for that particular individual (Joseph, 1995).

Detecting Untruthful Behavior

Verbal Characteristics of Potential Untruthful Behavior

Besides watching for nonverbal and physiological responses to help determine whether the interviewee may be untruthful, there are some verbal indicators that are often associated with either truthful or deceitful behavior. Note that these are *common* characteristics, and should only be used to assist the interviewer in determining baseline behavior. They should be used in conjunction with other interviewing and observational techniques, *not* as the sole reason to determine an untruth (Joseph, 1995):

1. A truthful person will give definitive answers; he or she will not qualify the response "Yes, I was there."
2. A deceitful person will qualify his or her answers.
3. A truthful person will be emphatic, or tell the interviewer that witnesses/fingerprints are wrong. A deceitful person will suggest that the interviewer *could* be wrong.
4. A truthful person will become angry when accused and will not calm easily or quickly.
5. A deceitful person will take a long time to answer questions; a truthful person will not.
6. A deceitful person will lie with specific details.

Verbal Lie Detector

There are three integral questions to ask as you close your interview. They are referred to as the "verbal lie detector." These questions coupled with information obtained from the interview help further evaluate information received during the process (Hess, 1997):

1. Did you do it? (Watch for reactions, body language, or denials.)
2. Have you told me everything?
3. Has everything you told me been the truth?

Interrogating Suspects

In a child abuse case, proper interrogation of a suspect may be instrumental in identifying the person responsible for the abuse of the child. Unless there is a videotape of the maltreatment (which is almost never the case), a suspect's voluntary confession of guilt or an excited utterance is probably the most powerful evidence that can be presented at trial. However, a suspect's written or electronically recorded voluntary statement is of little value unless it is admitted into evidence, which of course means that it must be obtained legally without violating the person's rights. The defense attorney will almost always challenge a suspect's confession by claiming coercion or some other violation of the client's rights under the 4th, 5th, 6th, or 14th constitutional amendment. Therefore, you must be thoroughly familiar with the case law in your state as it relates to obtaining confessions and the admissibility of confessions as evidence.

Ensure and *carefully document* that the suspect's constitutional rights are protected and that all applicable departmental procedures and state laws are followed. At a minimum, the case file should contain the following documentation:

- Whether the suspect was under arrest at the time of the questioning or was just brought in for an interview
- A note of when the interrogation started and how long it lasted. Videotape or tape recording is critical
- How often and at what time the suspect was allowed to use the restroom or to have something to eat or drink
- The names of any individuals who participated in the interview/interrogation or observed it
- Whether the suspect had any physical impairments, disabilities, or medical problems that could interfere with the ability to speak, hear, or understand what was being said. (If a person is legally deaf, state law may require the presence of a certified sign language interpreter.) Other disabilities should also be accommodated
- The suspect's level of formal education and whether the suspect can read and write.

Interrogate the suspect as early in the investigation as possible. You can usually begin as soon as the evidence indicates who the suspect is. The following guidelines will assist in conducting a proper interview/interrogation. Remember that when the interview begins to morph into an interrogation, you must Mirandize:

- Dress in business or casual clothes, not in a uniform. Do not wear a badge or carry a gun or handcuffs.
- If the suspect does not speak English and an interpreter is needed, make sure the interpreter is an expert in the suspect's language. This applies even when a law enforcement officer is used as an interpreter. Some states require that an individual pass a qualification test to be certified as an interpreter for legal

proceedings. The defense attorney may challenge the proficiency of any person used as an interpreter during an interrogation. An interpreter's incorrect use of one word can change the entire meaning of a sentence.

- Have another investigator observe the interrogation.
- If your agency does not videotape interrogations, the observer can rebut any allegations that you mistreated the suspect or coerced a confession. At least have a tape recording.
- If you cannot obtain a confession, the other investigator will be prepared to speak to the suspect. Observation allows the other investigator to know what the suspect has said and to reinforce, not contradict, what you have said. This "second bite at the apple" often results in a confession.
- Even if you cannot obtain a confession, document everything the suspect says. A suspect who does not confess may offer an explanation of surrounding events that is implausible or can be refuted by evidence. By documenting this unlikely account during the interrogation, you in effect lock the suspect into a story that can later be disproved or that will make the individual appear deceptive if he or she testifies in court.
- Always keep in mind that even if a suspect confesses, the confession may be suppressed at trial for a variety of procedural and legal reasons. That is one reason *you must not stop working on the case even if you obtain a confession.* Continue to investigate any new leads and interview anyone you think may have relevant information.

Tips and Reminders for Law Enforcement Investigators

1. An unreasonable delay in seeking medical attention is often a "red flag" that the child's injuries may have been caused by abuse.
2. Records of 911 calls often contain important information about what people originally reported regarding the allegations.
3. Always photo-document the crime scene.
4. Coordinate and communicate with CPS investigators in child abuse cases. They have the family involved. Each agency should notify the other agency when they are planning to speak with the suspect. This will let each agency have the same information.
5. The three keys to a successful child abuse investigation are effectively conducted, well-documented interviews of witnesses; careful background checks of everyone involved; and competent interview/interrogation of the suspect(s). The story must make sense and corroborate what you see at the scene and hear from the victim.
6. There is no substitute for a timely, professional crime scene search, including evidence collection, documentation, and photo-documentation. Even in cases

where there is delayed disclosure, it is critical to document the scene and search for physical evidence.

7. If criminal charges are filed, properly prepare for your courtroom testimony and deliver it competently.

Perpetrator Characteristics

Who abuses and neglects children? A perpetrator is the person who is responsible for the abuse or neglect of a child. For federal fiscal year 2012, fifty states reported 512,040 unique perpetrators. The unique count tallies a perpetrator only once, regardless of the number of times the perpetrator is associated with maltreating a child.

Generally, we think of two types of perpetrators in child sexual molestation cases: the "preferential" offender who actually prefers children and has particular "type" in mind and the "situational" offender who does not necessarily have a preference for children but finds himself in a situation to offend. This type of perpetrator has difficulty with adult relationships.

According to the US Department of Health and Human Services (2013), the following analyses were conducted using a unique count of perpetrators:

- Four-fifths (82.2%) of perpetrators were between the ages of 18 and 44 years.
- More than one-half (53.5%) of perpetrators were women, 45.3% of perpetrators were men, and 1.1% were of unknown sex. Using a duplicated count of perpetrators, meaning a perpetrator is counted each time the same perpetrator is associated with maltreating a child, the total duplicated count of perpetrators was 893,659.
- For 2012, four-fifths (80.3%) of duplicated perpetrators were parents.
- Of the duplicated perpetrators who were parents, 88.5% were the biological parents.

The National Child Abuse and Neglect Data System (NCANDS) define a perpetrator as a person who was determined to have caused or knowingly allowed the maltreatment of a child. NCANDS does not collect information about persons who were alleged to be perpetrators and not found to have perpetrated abuse and neglect.

As states have improved their child welfare information systems, perpetrators have received unique identifiers within CPS agency databases. The unique identifiers enable NCANDS to count perpetrators two ways:

- *Duplicated count of perpetrators*: Counting a perpetrator each time the perpetrator is associated with maltreating a child. This also is known as a report–child–perpetrator triad. For example, the same perpetrator would be counted twice in all of the following situations: (1) one child in two separate reports, (2) two children in a single report, and (3) two children in two separate reports.

- *Unique count of perpetrators*: Identifying and counting a perpetrator once, regardless of the number of children the perpetrator is associated with maltreating or the number of records associated with a perpetrator. For federal fiscal year 2012, 50 states reported a unique count of 512,040 perpetrators.

Perpetrator demographics (unique count of perpetrators): From the Best Practices *Child Maltreatment 2012* report, the perpetrator age groups were changed to display the proportions of perpetrators by age and to categorize perpetrators who were legal adults (meaning older than 17 years) and those who were minors.

- More than four-fifths (82.2%) of perpetrators were between the ages of 18 and 44 years inclusive.
- Two-fifths (39.6%) of perpetrators were in the 25–34 years age group,
- 23.4% were in the 35–44 years age group.
- One-fifth (19.2%) were in the 18–24 years age group.
- Perpetrators younger than 18 years accounted for fewer than 3% of all perpetrators.
- More than one-half (53.5%) of perpetrators were women.
- 45.3% of perpetrators were men.
- 1.1% were of unknown sex.
- The racial distributions of perpetrators were similar to the race of their victims.
- The three largest percentages of perpetrators were whites (48.9%).
- African-American (19.9%).
- Hispanic (18.9%) racial or ethnic descent.
- Race or ethnicity was not reported for 8.7% of perpetrators.

Perpetrator relationship victim data were analyzed by relationship of victims (duplicate count) to their perpetrators.

- Four-fifths (81.5%) of victims were maltreated by one or both parent(s).
- The parent(s) could have acted together, acted alone, or acted with up to two other people to maltreat the child.
- Nearly two-fifths (36.6%) of victims were maltreated by their mother acting alone.
- One-fifth (18.7%) of victims were maltreated by their father acting alone.
- One-fifth (19.4%) of victims were maltreated by both parents.
- 12% of victims were maltreated by a perpetrator who was not the child's parent.

Reviewing 911 Emergency Calls

A 911 call for assistance in the child abuse or child fatality case under investigation may provide important information about the event. Keep in mind that more than one call may have come in about the same incident. The 911 computer records indicate the exact time and location of the call. Most 911 systems electronically record the conversations. You can listen to an audio copy of the call and hear exactly what the caller said. Often in maltreatment injuries or deaths, the caller actually caused the child's injuries, and there will be significant discrepancies between what that person said in the 911 call and what he or she says later in an interview.

The 911 call will also help to determine the following:

- *Identity.* Even if the caller does not give a name, you may recognize the voice during a subsequent interview. In some cases, in which callers left the scene before first responders arrived, the recorded calls were the only proof they were at the location and somehow involved.
- *Reason for calling.* The caller may have said whether the child was sick, injured, unconscious, or deceased. Callers may contradict themselves in a subsequent interview.
- *Exact words.* Listen to how the caller describes the child's condition and the events and circumstances leading up to the phone call (e.g., the child fell down a flight of stairs and is now unconscious, or the caller found the child unconscious and knows nothing about the cause).
- *Emotional state.* Tone of voice and choice of words may reveal the caller's emotional state. The caller may express remorse for his or her actions.
- *Other people at the location.* It may be possible to determine whether other people were present when the call was made. Even if they do not talk on the phone, the caller may talk to them or mention their names or their voices may be audible in the background.
- *Review 911 tapes*

Know the procedures of your 911 emergency call center or agency dispatcher. Almost all agencies erase tapes or digital recordings of emergency calls after a certain period of time, so be sure to obtain copies before the recordings you need are destroyed. (Again, keep in mind that more than one person may have called 911 about the incident in question, or the same person may have called more than once.) After obtaining a copy from the call center, make a backup copy for work purposes and keep the original copy in the file. If you are using a cassette tape, remove the tabs that allow a tape to be recorded to prevent accidentally taping over the conversation you need. You may also consider having a written transcript made of the 911 call, which will make it easier to locate specific statements during subsequent interviews and interrogations.

Checklist of Potential Information Sources

- CPS records (for the child, siblings, or other children that the child's caretakers have been involved with).
- Law enforcement records (criminal history, victim or suspect history, or calls for service).
- Medical records for the child and siblings (birth, prenatal care, pediatrician, medical, emergency room, and so on).
- 911 calls.
- Emergency medical services (EMS) reports.
- Telephone calls that the suspect made or received around the time of the child's injury (including cell phones, pagers, or messages on answering machines).
- Autopsy results for all child deaths.

Important records documenting a history of abuse or neglect may exist in cities, towns, or states where the child's family or the suspect previously lived.

Learning from the Autopsy

Remember, for babies and children who die, there must be a clearly documented medical history or documentation for a thoroughly investigated accidental injury to substantiate a natural or accidental death of a child. Child Fatality Review Boards are extremely important and a good example of the MDT approach. These teams of law enforcement, medical professionals, solicitors, CPS workers, and others involved in the welfare and protection of children can be a valuable asset in reviewing practices and protocols and for making improvements in the prevention and investigation of child abuse cases.

The autopsy will determine the official cause of death (blunt force trauma, drowning, and so on) and manner of death (natural, accidental, homicide, suicide, and undetermined). You should observe the autopsy if at all possible. The information learned from the autopsy will better prepare you for subsequent interviews and interrogations.

The pathologist can provide information about the child's injuries, including those related to the death and those previously inflicted, and about the child's general state of health prior to death. It is important to ask the pathologist to explain whether a single event or multiple factors caused or contributed to the death. Additionally, based on the injuries, the pathologist or a pediatrician may be able to say how the child would have reacted after being injured—for example, whether the child would have been able to walk or talk, been in obvious pain, or lost consciousness.

Another important question to ask is when the child's symptoms would have first appeared. The answers to these questions may help you determine whether witness accounts are truthful. In turn, you can tell the pathologist what you have learned from your interviews and record checks. In many cases, the pathologist can offer an opinion regarding the possibility that the child's injuries occurred in the manner described by witnesses. The pathologist may also be able to estimate the time of death, based on stomach contents and your notes about the child's last meal.

The Decision-Making Process

The investigator is responsible for making a number of significant decisions including those that pertain to a finding regarding the allegation; the child's safety; the child's placement; and supports and services necessary for the child, foster family, or birth family during the investigation. The decision to substantiate a report must be based on clearly defined, consistent criteria. Different states use different criteria. It is important that criteria across states are consistent and straightforward. Reliable assessment tools that guide decision making and protocols that standardize best practices create the most appropriate responses. Due to the investigator's specialized training, objectivity, and lack of ongoing case responsibility, it is important that this critical determination is the primary responsibility of the investigator. In all decision making, however, the investigator should solicit input, consultation, and supervision to inform and guide the process.

Putting the Pieces Together

Witnesses typically provide information about an event or circumstance. Due to the fact that there is a tendency for witnesses to talk about what they have seen and to "compare notes," it is always advisable to separate them prior to conducting interviews. The purpose of an interview is to obtain truthful information, and if witnesses have been influenced by each other's statements, a vital piece of information or observation may be lost.

Take into consideration that perceptions of size and color can vary greatly from witness to witness. Size is relative. A person 5′ 10″ tall may be perceived as short by a person 6′ tall, but would probably be considered as of average height to someone 5′ 8″ or even 5′ 10″. Most witnesses are honest, but they are human and are susceptible to outside influences, biases, and prejudgments. It is a good practice to interview all parties separately to avoid potential problems.

Investigators should use caution when taking a victim or witness back to a crime scene for an on-the-scene suspect identification. This procedure may seem practical based on the time constraints and the nature of the crime, but should rarely be used in order to protect the crime scene and the victim's identity. Prior to engaging in such practices officers should consult with a supervisor to ensure that this technique is necessary. A photo array (line-up) may be a more practical way for the victim to identify the suspect, particularly if the victim has experienced some form of extreme trauma.

Documenting the Scene

The amount of documentation and the type of documentation may vary somewhat depending on the totality of circumstances at the scene. A death investigation will take more documentation but nonetheless, an abuse case will need much of the same documentation. Photographs of injuries can tell us a lot about what may happened to the child. Specific pattern injuries can often tell us the type of weapon that was used, even in some cases if it was a physical assault with only the offender's hands. We can find fingertip bruises, fingernail marks, scratches, and abrasions. An evidence-establishing shot of the injury in relationship to anatomical body landmarks can give a good overall picture of the injuries sustained. Then, a close-up of the specific injuries should be taken. Use a scale to indicate size.

Scene Photos

We want to tell the story of what happened and what we saw at the scene. If or when the case goes to court, photographic evidence can be a key witness. Appropriate scene photography is to take a series of three types of photographs: Distant, mid-range, and close-up. Distant photos are taken to get an overview of the entire scene setting. Take them from a 360° perspective. Overlap about 25% of the edge in each photo. This will give a clear picture of the area. These photos are typically taken at the boundary of the scene itself. Next, mid-range photos are taken. These are also called evidence-establishing shots because they show evidence in relationship to other items at the scene. Move up about half-way to the evidence you have. Take a photo from that vantage point and from a four corners approach to get various angles. This is to show the relationship of the evidence to some landmark in the scene. The next and last series of photos is taken just before the evidence is collected. Take a close-up of the item as you find it, in place at the scene. Take it with and without a scale in the photo. This will allow you to keep the relative size perspective when it is blown up for court purposes. Take the close-up so that the item completely fills the frame of the photo. Be sure to take it with a close-up lens and focus to record any particular detail. Take several from different angles. Later, if it is laboratory evidence or forensic evidence that is examined, additional photos can be taken.

Sketching the Scene

A sketch of the scene is nice to have in some abuse cases it may not be necessary, but if there is evidence at the scene it may be helpful to have and should be mandatory in child death investigations. It is easier to get a black and white sketch into court rather than certain crime scene photos. Sketching the scene can be a valuable asset to the investigation and in court. A rough sketch should be drawn at the scene and can later be drawn to scale and nicely diagrammed for court. In order to be used in court a sketch has two requirements: it must be an accurate representation of the scene and it must be part of the testimony of a qualified witness. That is why it is important to write on the sketch the name of the person who drew it and the address of the scene for jurisdictional purposes. If the scene is indoors, say the bedroom of a residence, sketch the bedroom separately. Also sketch a floor plan of the entire house and designate the location of that bedroom clearly on the overall floor plan. The rough sketch does not have to be to scale, but a final sketch will be a scale drawing. Therefore, you should indicate the measurement of the perimeter, or the room where the scene took place so that a scale drawing can be made later. A sketch has many uses (Weston and Lushbaugh, 2006):

1. It can record the location of evidence.
2. It can supplement photographs and can create a picture for the judge, jury, and attorney.
3. It can refresh memories about the scene and may be used to show the jury in lieu of bloody photographs.

4. It can create a permanent record of the scene and establish relationships between evidence.

Sketches must contain basic information:

1. The layout of the scene, floor plan, or crime scene area.
2. Exact location for jurisdictional purposes.
3. Names of anyone assisting with or drawing the sketch.
4. Case number.
5. Legend or key with evidence marked as numbers and non-evidentiary items as letters.
6. Directional north.

Rough sketches are not drawn to scale and a scale is not necessary but the measurements or plotting of the evidence must be accurate. Later a scale drawing can be made and the scale must be noted. The agency should have a protocol for when sketches will be drawn. All homicides should have a scene sketch.

Always keep your rough draft. If something is inadvertently omitted in the final sketch, it can be called into evidence as well as the final sketch.

First, lay out the perimeter or basic floor plan if indoors. Then add the fixed objects like street lights and furniture. Once those items are added, put in the evidence. Rough sketches do not have to be to scale. Major items of evidence should be placed in the sketch and the measurements of the evidence in relation to other objects must be accurate. A final sketch will be drawn to scale later if needed.

Three useful types of crime scene sketches (Weston and Lushbaugh, 2006) are as follows:

1. Overview also known as the bird's eye view

This is a sketch as if you were looking straight down on the scene. It is a basic floor plan type of sketch and can be used indoors or outdoors. First draw the perimeter of the scene and put in the items of nonevidentiary value such as furniture, trees, and pond. Then place the evidence in the scene. Use letters for items of non-evidentiary value and numbers for items of evidence. This type of sketch is the simplest and most common type of sketch drawn. It can be used when the evidence of interest lies in one plane. The general progression of drawing a sketch is to lay out the basic perimeter and set the fixed objects such as fence posts, trees, or building corners. Next, insert the evidence as it is recovered and record the appropriate measurements. Finally, label the key, the legend, the compass north, and other items on the sketch.

2. Elevation sketch

The elevation drawing is used when the vertical rather than the horizontal plane is of interest. (Examples: if blood spatter is present on a wall; determining the path of a projectile.)

3. Cross-projection sketch

The cross-projection drawing is similar to the floor plan sketch, except the walls have been folded down into the same plane as the floor. This allows objects to be shown on the walls and floor in the same drawing. It combines the bird's eye sketch with the elevation sketch.

Searching the Scene

After photographing and sketching a scene, the officer should search the scene for physical evidence. Hopefully, there will be several officers to assist in the search if the scene is large, but remember that only one office should bag and tag the evidence for chain of custody purposes.

There are several ways to search a crime scene and while no one method is the best in every case, there are certain patterns that are more appropriate for the terrain. Remember, there is only one chance to get this right. Always record the names of the searchers. In some cases of missing persons and volunteer community search groups, the suspect may participate to insert themselves into the investigation. The best way to search a scene is with a warrant. After completing a protective sweep of the area a search warrant should be obtained. It may be necessary to post an officer at the scene to secure it until the warrant is received. Always keep copies of the warrant in the case file, or, in cases of consent, get it in writing and preferably on camera or videotape. Always record the evidence collected and leave a copy of the items seized at the residence listing those things were secured during the search.

Photograph all areas before beginning the search. Searching a vehicle should follow the same guidelines. Photograph the entire vehicle including the tires straight on to see the tread pattern. Note the identifying information about the vehicle, tag, VIN, make model, color, registration number, odometer reading, and any damage to the vehicle. If towed, the company name and address and the driver name. Who accompanied the vehicle?

There are four basic patterns that should meet most needs for crime scene searches (Weston and Lushbaugh, 2006):

1. Parallel search pattern—Good for large areas and several searchers. All team members form a single line, usually fingertip to fingertip and walk in the

same direction at the same time from one end of the crime scene to the other. When evidence is found it is called out and a marker is put down. Then the team continues forward.

2. Grid search pattern—Good for large areas and several searchers. This is basically two parallel searches done at right angles. First, the searchers start out with a parallel search as described above. Then, when they reach the end of the search area, the team starts at the side boundary and searches at a 90° angle thereby covering the same area again in a 90° direction. Everyone moves in the same direction at the same time and then turns at a right angle and searches forming a grid pattern.
3. Inward spiral search pattern—Good when there is only one officer available to search an area. The inward spiral starts at the perimeter of the scene and moves inward to the center. The officer begins the search at a specific location on the outer perimeter of the secured area. Walking along the entire perimeter of the scene the officer searches for evidence. When found, a marker is put down. When the officer reaches the same spot where he began, he steps two feet inward and continues around the perimeter again. When he has made a complete circle and returns to the starting point, he steps inward two feet again and continues the search until reaching the center of the scene, forming an inward spiral. Starting at the outside perimeter and moving inward allows for less contamination than starting at the focal point and moving outward.
4. Zone or sector search pattern—Good for areas that are naturally divided or those that can be readily divided into sectors. Searching vehicles is a good example. The passenger compartment is one zone, the hood and the trunk are other zones, and the undercarriage is yet another zone. Each team member takes a zone and searches it. If this is a large area, several searchers may search a single zone using whatever pattern inside the zone best suits the location. Team members may then switch locations or zones, and the area can be re-searched with a fresh pair of eyes to ensure good coverage. In large areas to be searched, each zone may use an appropriate search pattern.

Plotting Methods

There are three ways to measure or plot evidence at the scene (Weston and Lushbaugh, 2006):

1. Triangulation method

This is the most common type of plotting method used. It can be employed anywhere, indoors or outdoors. The method requires two fixed reference points to locate the position of objects. (Example: if the crime scene is in a room, objects can be located by using the corners of the room.) Objects are then located and recorded by the distance from the two points. Using the head of the body as one, the north corner of the shed as A, the south corner B, the two trees as C and D, and the fence post as E and F, we can plot the position of the body using two of the stationary items plotted to a body position.

2. Rectangular coordinates methods

This method requires two reference points at right angles to each other and is often used to locate objects in a room. Two walls of the room serve as the lines and the distances are then measured from the object to each of the walls along a line perpendicular (at right angles) to the wall.

3. Baseline method

This method requires measurements to be taken along and from a single reference line called the baseline. This line should be established by the use of a string, chalk line, or some convenient means prior to any measurements being made. Often the line is established between two objects (trees, utility poles, or between two corners of a room). One end of the line is selected as the starting point and objects are located by giving the distance from the starting point along this line to a point opposite to the object, and then from the object to the baseline along a perpendicular line to the baseline.

Physical Evidence

Physical evidence is any material, however microscopic, solid, liquid, or gaseous that may aid in the determination of the truth during the investigation of a crime. Saferstein, 2004, p. 35, defines physical evidence as "any object that can establish that a crime has been committed or can provide a link between a crime and its victim or between a crime and its perpetrator." Physical evidence can take many forms: solid, liquid, or gaseous. It can be very large or microscopic. It can be found on the victim, the suspect, and at the scene. It may be transferred to other objects or even other locations. Depending on the type of scene, the evidence or the lack of expected evidence may tell the investigator a great deal about the crime and the perpetrator and the victim. The importance of a thorough and methodical search for evidence is the key to aiding in the investigation, arrest, and conviction of the perpetrator.

The evidence observed at a crime scene has the potential to be a valuable tool in the investigation and apprehension of a suspect, and realization of this potential depends on actions taken early on at the crime scene. "Investigators should approach the crime scene as if it will be their only opportunity to preserve and recover these physical clues" (Crime Scene Investigation: A Guide for Law Enforcement, 2000, p. 1). Physical evidence collected at these crime scenes is normally tangible and provides impartial facts. An item of physical evidence cannot be cross examined, although its chain of custody and freedom from contamination may be attacked. The documentation, presentation, and evaluation of physical evidence can provide a valuable contribution in court cases, if the evidence is collected and handled properly, beginning with the first responder and continuing throughout the chain of custody. Once these requirements are met, evidence is no longer "silent" and will facilitate the ability of the prosecutor and jury to interpret a story supported by physical evidence. As will be discussed later, if used effectively, the evidence could overcome a series of conflicting and confusing statements offered by witnesses who observed the same incident at essentially the same time.

Classification of Evidence

During a criminal trial, two kinds of proofs are used to answer the question of guilt or innocence:

1. *Direct evidence*: this involves eyewitnesses who have, through one or more of their five senses, experienced something relative to the crime or its circumstances (Weston, 2006, p. 25).
2. *Circumstantial evidence*: on the other hand, this is evidence from which an inference can be drawn and includes physical evidence such as a weapon, blood, and impressions (Weston, 2006, p. 25). This is the majority of our evidence! If wet clothing, package in paper.

In addition, physical evidence has certain characteristics that may help to link it to the crime scene, victim, or suspect, or corroborate the victim's statements. In child sexual abuse cases, child victims may describe different types of physical evidence that may bring credibility to their statements. Even when there is delayed disclosure, this evidence may still exist, and can include:

1. Minute/latent evidence—This consists of trace amounts of bodily fluids (e.g., semen, blood, or saliva), pubic hair, fibers, or skin cells located on

bedding, linens, clothes, cloth furniture, carpet, or at the scene where the alleged incident occurred.

2. Lures—In cases of child sexual abuse, offenders often use gifts to entice the child into a situation or try to maintain their interest. This can come in the form of toys, electronics, clothes, music, or special events, like a trip to an amusement park, concert, or sporting event.
3. Adult pornography—In their efforts to groom their victims, offenders often use adult pornography to "educate" or desensitize them to sexually explicit information.
4. Child pornography—The offender may possess child pornography for their own pleasure, or as a means to normalize child sexual behaviors.
5. Souvenirs—Offenders oftentimes collect keepsakes as reminders of their contact with their victims. This can include undergarments, personal items, nonsexual photos of the victim, and ticket stubs from events they have attended together.
6. Sexual aids/devices—Children may describe the use of sexual aids or devices used by the offender during the act, such as a lubricant, petroleum jelly, condoms, sex toys, or bondage items.
7. Drugs/alcohol—Offenders may knowingly or unknowingly provide drugs or alcohol to their victims. This may include over-the-counter sleep aids, antihistamines, illegal drugs, or various alcoholic beverages.

Chain of Custody and Its Importance

A chain of custody is a permanent record of all persons who have handled the piece of evidence since it was collected at the scene. A proper chain of custody must accompany each item of evidence collected at the scene. To be a proper chain of custody it must give the history of every person who handled the evidence from the time of collection to the time of court testimony. Appropriate packaging material must secure the evidence and the date, and scene or case number, and the collector's name or initials must be on the packaging preventing tampering with the item. When the laboratory receives the evidence it is logged in and logged out to a specific examiner for testing. The package is usually opened from another area in order to leave the original evidence sealing tape in place so that the collector can identify it in court. The laboratory then reseals it, and dates and initials it when completed. Remember that a paper chain of custody is necessary for the item to be admitted in court.

Medical Evidence

DNA Evidence

Blood Serology and DNA

Blood also has class characteristics. When two samples are compared, it can be determined that both are human and both are Type A. For example, if the frequency of occurrence in the population of Type A blood is 26%, then this would not be enough to establish a common source. However, if analyzed further and other blood factors are found in common, the probability of the two sources originating from the same common source increases (Saferstein, 2004, p. 67). Today, technology enables the forensic scientist to analyze blood, semen, saliva, and other biologicals, compare an unknown to a known, and individualize the specimen to a particular person.

Saliva is often compared as secretor or non-secretor. Semen can be used for DNA matches as well as other bodily fluids. Touch DNA is possible and epithelial or skin cell matches are possible.

CODIS (COmbined DNA Index System) is a nationwide database of DNA profiles. There are two sections in the system: one is an offender area which has DNA profiles of known offenders; the other is an unknown area where the DNA owner is unknown but the DNA was found at a crime scene. Both are important and can be helpful. Standards will also have to be submitted for comparison. Hair samples should include the root (follicular tag) depending on the laboratory guidelines, whenever possible.

Trace evidence is also an important component of many cases and can link the suspect or offender to the victim and to a location. Trace evidence includes material such as hairs, fibers, soil, and other debris that may link the offender with the victim.

What Happens After a Report Is Made (Caveats for Jurisdictions)

When the initial report is made, the information is reviewed and when the intake criteria are met, the case is either "founded" or "unfounded." These terms may vary but in essence the case is accepted or not.

Screening of Referrals

A referral may be either screened in or screened out. Reasons for screening out a referral vary by state policy, but may include one or more of the following:

- Did not meet the state's intake standard
- Did not concern child abuse and neglect
- Did not contain enough information for a CPS response to occur
- Response by another agency was deemed more appropriate
- Children in the referral were the responsibility of another agency or jurisdiction (e.g., military installation or tribe).

Most states define a child as a person who has not yet reached their 18th birthday. CPS agencies across the nation receive millions of referrals each year. The national FFY 2012 estimate of 3.4 million referrals involves 6.3 million children, including duplicate counts (US Department of Health and Human Services).

When an investigation response results in a determination (also known as a disposition) about the alleged child maltreatment, there are several possibilities. Two of the most prevalent dispositions are:

- *Substantiated*: An investigation disposition that concludes that the allegation of maltreatment or risk of maltreatment was supported or founded by state law or policy.
- *Unsubstantiated*: An investigation disposition that determines that there was not sufficient evidence under state law to conclude or suspect that the child was maltreated or at-risk of being maltreated.
- Less commonly used dispositions for investigation responses include:
  - *Indicated*: A disposition that concludes that maltreatment could not be substantiated under state law or policy, but there was reason to suspect that at least one child may have been maltreated or was at-risk of maltreatment. This is applicable only to states that distinguish between substantiated and indicated dispositions.
  - *Intentionally false*: A disposition that indicates a conclusion that the person who made the allegation of maltreatment knew that the allegation was not true.
  - *Closed with no finding or unsubstantiated*: A disposition that does not conclude with a specific finding because the CPS response could not be completed. This disposition is often assigned when CPS is unable to locate the alleged victim.
  - *Other*: States may also use the category of "other," if none of the above is applicable. Several states use this disposition when the results of an

investigation are "uncertain," "inconclusive," or "unable to be determined." State statutes also establish the level of evidence needed to determine a disposition of substantiated or indicated (see Appendix C for each state's level of evidence). These statutes influence how CPS agencies respond to the safety needs of the children who are the subjects of child maltreatment reports.

Alternative Response

In some states, reports of maltreatment may not be investigated but are instead assigned to an alternative track, often called alternative response, family assessment response (FAR), or differential response (DR). Cases assigned this response often include early determinations that the children have a low risk of maltreatment. Alternative responses usually include the voluntary acceptance of CPS services and the mutual agreement of family needs. These cases usually do not result in a formal determination regarding the maltreatment allegation or alleged perpetrator.

While families who receive an alternative response do not receive a finding such as "preponderance of evidence" or "unsubstantiated" as would be the case in an investigation of abuse, the term "disposition" is used for both investigative and alternative responses. Each state that uses alternative response decides how to map its codes for these programs in relation to these NCANDS codes:

Alternative response victim: The provision of a response other than an investigation that determines that a child was a victim of maltreatment. Three states report children in this category, referring to cases where the CPS agency or the courts required the family to receive services.

Alternative response non-victim: The provision of a response other than an investigation that did not determine that a child was a victim of maltreatment.

Variations in how states define and implement alternative response programs continue to emerge. For example, several states mentioned in their commentary (Appendix D) have an alternative response program that is not reported to NCANDS. These states are Alabama, Arkansas, California, Connecticut, Hawaii, Maine, North Dakota, Pennsylvania, Rhode Island, and South Dakota. For some of these states, the alternative response programs provide services for families regardless of whether or not there were any allegations of child maltreatment. Another reason why alternative response program data may not be reported to NCANDS is that the program may not be implemented statewide.

To test implementation feasibility, states often first pilot or rollout programs in select counties. Two additional states—Iowa and Maryland—commented that an alternative response program is in development and may be implemented in the coming years; however, it is not yet known whether these two states will report the alternative response data to NCANDS. Readers are encouraged to review Appendix D for more information about these programs (Best Practice Guidelines for Child Maltreatment in Foster Care, 2003).

Criminal Background Checks

Run criminal background checks as early as possible at the beginning of the investigation. It may be possible to do so while on scene and to allow CPS to place the child with a family member then and there. Each agency should run criminal records checks on all individuals who were involved with the immediate care of the child or anyone present at the time of abuse or injury. Check Child Protection Agency history and Sex Offender Registry databases. In child fatality cases, interview siblings and others in the household. Interview teachers, counselors, activity coaches, and neighbors.

Post-Investigation Response by CPS Agency

When a CPS worker substantiates a report, the child welfare team needs to make important placement decisions regarding the reported child and other children residing in the home:

- Are all children in the home currently safe?
- Has the investigation successfully addressed all safety and risk factors?
- Are children connected by strong positive relationships to the family or caregiver?

The team must make decisions as to the future status of the home:

- If the child is in a foster home when the allegation is received, should the foster home be closed? If not, what type of corrective plan is necessary to address ongoing risk factors?
- How can the team address systemic factors that may have contributed to the maltreatment to prevent further concerns about the care of children residing

in the home? Other concerns may exist and require attention when reports do not reach the statutory threshold to be considered maltreatment:

- Are there concerns about the parents' ability to provide an acceptable standard of care that should be addressed through the investigation process?
- What type of corrective plan is necessary to address those concerns?
- Are there placement issues that the worker must address to avoid further reports of maltreatment?

Important Activities

These activities include:

- Clearly tell the parents, if the child or children are removed from the home either through emergency protective action or other, what they must do before the children can be returned.
- Provide follow-up and support to the child, the birth family, and the foster family if the child is placed in a foster care home, for services that have been identified as necessary.
- Determine what services or treatment plan is in place to address the issues discovered through the investigation and specifically who is responsible for the follow-up.

Finally, although the investigation must focus primarily on child safety, all parties must be aware that the report of maltreatment and subsequent investigation can negatively affect children's stability, permanency, and well-being. Each of the decisions and tasks is significant, and different members of the child welfare team will have unique roles in carrying them out. Clearly, this phase of the investigation is one in which teamwork continues to be essential and the MDT approach is particularly helpful.

Decisions and Tasks Following a Substantiated Investigation

The first consideration following a determination of maltreatment is the safety of the child and other children living in the home. Safety assessment is an ongoing process that begins with the start of the investigation and continues as the worker gathers more extensive information regarding the allegations, the caregivers, and the child. With the conclusion of the investigation, in addition to safety, other long-term decisions regarding permanence must be made. Children need to be in settings where caregivers meet their developmental needs and provide them with nurturing and supportive adult relationships.

Along with safety, those criteria must be met as well if children are to remain with the family or if placed in a foster setting following a substantiated investigation.

Under the following circumstances it is safe for a child to remain with their family following a substantiated investigation:

- When the adult responsible for the maltreatment is no longer living in the home and will not have access to the children living in the foster home.
- When the parents can ensure that the behavior of a maltreating child who continues to reside in the home can be safely controlled within the home setting and that the level of supervision is adequate to ensure no unsupervised contact with other children.
- When the level of maltreatment was less serious and less harmful than indicated by statutory threshold and the person responsible has demonstrated the necessary emotional and behavioral control to ensure that it will not occur again.
- When formal risk assessment indicates that the risk of future maltreatment in the home is low.
- In the case of foster parents, when the child has a strong attachment to the foster parents, feels comfortable and safe, and wants to remain in the foster home and when the relationship between the child and foster family has the goal of permanence (the child is in a pre-adoptive or kinship home) and all of the above conditions are met.

In short, a child should only remain in the home when it is clearly safe and in the child's best interests to do so. This complex decision must be made through a group decision-making process that includes input from all members of the child welfare team, including the child and family service worker, foster parent in foster situations, the child, child's family, and key supervisory and administrative staff. The decision must be based on a thorough knowledge of the family, if foster care applies—the foster home setting, and the child.

When the above conditions are met, and it is deemed to be safe and in the child's best interests to remain in the home:

- the agency should be responsible for closely monitoring and working with the parents to address any ongoing concerns or risk factors;
- the a gency's contacts with the parents and the child should be increased and the situation carefully monitored;
- the agency should help the family attain any outside supports and services, such as parenting skills, treatment services, and health care, needed to address any concerns.

Again, these decisions are not simple ones, and they can have significant consequences for the child and family involved. Thus, they should be made with the benefit of sound group decision-making processes. Finally, systemic factors can increase the stress on vulnerable parents and workers should consider these factors in the assessment, decision making, and follow-up with families.

Such families may have less coping capacity than families receiving the supports and services they need to effectively take on the challenging task of caring for children with serious needs. In such situations, the child welfare team should address these factors to prevent unnecessary stress for families providing care especially when a child in the home has a disability (Best Practice Guidelines for Child Maltreatment in Foster Care, 2003).

Decisions and Tasks Following an Unsubstantiated Investigation

Reports of maltreatment may be unsubstantiated for various reasons:

- The worker determines that an allegation was false.
- The reports were made by well-meaning people whose observations concerned them, but further investigation documented that no maltreatment occurred. In these types of situations, the safety of the children living in the home has been ensured.
- Concerns remain about the possibility of maltreatment or the level of care provided in the home, yet the worker finds insufficient evidence to substantiate the report, or the behaviors of concern do not reach the threshold of maltreatment.

Each of these situations involves unique challenges for the child welfare team.

When Concerns Remain

When the reported incident or behavior does not reach the level of maltreatment but raises concerns about the standard of care in the home, these concerns should be addressed by the agency or through services and treatment options:

- If concerns about the child's welfare remain, the investigator should immediately share the concerns with designated staff, the family, and the supervisor who works directly with the family.

- The worker should clearly identify the issues and develop and monitor a corrective plan to address those issues.
- Decisions regarding continued placement should be based on an assessment that the child is safe and that the home effectively addresses the child's needs. When this is not the case, a different placement should be considered.

When, during the course of the investigation, the investigator has reason to suspect that someone has maltreated birth- or adoptive children living in the foster home, those parties with direct information should file a report of maltreatment with the CPS agency, and the agency should initiate an independent investigation.

Notifications

State statutes and policies identify those parties that should receive notice, and statutes provide time frames by which the notification of the investigative decision should occur. Notification of key parties of the investigation outcome should be done in accordance with those provisions. In investigating families, the following parties should be notified:

- Child and family service workers with ongoing responsibility for the child and other children in the home
- Foster parents, if applicable
- Family workers, birth- or adoptive parents of the reported child, and other children in the home
- The reported child and other children in the home
- The law enforcement agency, when a law enforcement investigation is ongoing or serious concerns exist that merit a referral to law enforcement
- The tribal social service office, if the child or family is American-Indian
- The mandated reporter.

At the conclusion of the investigation, the child welfare team should conduct a number of activities to ensure the child's safety, stabilize relationships, and minimize the trauma the child might experience from placement transitions. The team must make important decisions regarding the ongoing status of the foster family as a placement resource for the child.

Key principles employed throughout the intake and investigation process continue to shape decision-making and casework activities at its conclusion:

- The child's need for safety, permanence, and well-being guide all decisions and case activities.

- All members of the child welfare team have essential responsibilities during this process.
- Decisions of this magnitude must be based on sound information gathered from multiple sources through a disciplined and systematic process.
- Decisions should rarely be the responsibility of one person and should be shared by key members of the child welfare team.
- The agency should treat everyone involved in the process with respect and include them to the greatest degree possible.
- The agency should make all efforts to minimize the trauma and disruption that children, birth families, and foster families experience during this process (Best Practice Guidelines for Child Maltreatment in Foster Care, 2003).

These principles are intended to serve as a reference or guideline for the development of sound child abuse investigative principles. Although some of the items listed are from the Best Practice Guidelines for Child Maltreatment in Foster Care, many of the principles also apply to children who are not currently in foster care. For example: The Crime Scene Sketch.

Notifications

Contact	Action	Rationale
Child welfare worker	Immediately notify through personal contact followed by formal written notification	Share all information to make accurate determination of safety and risk for children
Pre-adoptive parents or foster parent	Notify as soon as possible following the completion of the investigation	Provide opportunity to discuss decision, debrief, and explore implications of outcomes for their families, and children placed in their home
Ongoing family foster care or licensing/ certification worker	Immediately notify of investigation decision and all information necessary to help determine ongoing status of foster family and development of corrective plan	Provide with opportunity to discuss maltreatment and concerns for their children; keep informed of ongoing efforts to ensure safety and well-being of their children; provide ongoing support

Reported child and other children in the home	Participate in joint meetings with key members of child welfare team	Provide with information and support
Law enforcement investigator	Immediately notify of investigation outcome and concerns as well as any action taken to protect safety and well-being of children residing in home	Share all information relevant to law enforcement investigation and possible criminal violation
Mandated reporter	Notify according to state statutes and policies	Provide information regarding the decision, reason to accept or not accept the report, and the reason to substantiate or not substantiate if the report is accepted

References

American Professional Society on the Abuse of Children, 2012. Practice Guidelines: Forensic Interviewing in Cases of Suspected Child Abuse. American Professional Society on the Abuse of Children, Chicago, IL.

Best Practice Guidelines for Child Maltreatment in Foster Care, 2003. Child Welfare League of America, Inc.

Crime Scene Investigation: A Guide for Law Enforcement, 2000. US Department of Justice. Washington, DC.

Hess, J.E., 1997. Interviewing and Interrogation for Law Enforcement. Anderson Publishing Company, Reading, UK.

Innocence Project. (http://www.innocenceproject.org/understand/Eyewitness-Misidentification.php).

Joseph Jr., A.J., 1995. We Get Confessions. Printing Methods, Inc., New York.

Reid, J.E., Associates, 2008. The Reid Technique of Interviewing and Interrogation®.

Saferstein, R., 2004. Criminalistics: An Introduction to Forensic Science. Prentice Hall, Upper Saddle River, NJ.

The Crime Scene Sketch. (http://www.bcps.org/offices/science/secondary/forensic/Crimescene%20Sketch.pdf).

US Department of Health and Human Services, Administration for Children and Families, Administration on Children, Youth and Families, Children's Bureau, 2013. Child Maltreatment 2012. Available from http://www.acf.hhs.gov/programs/cb/research-data-technology/statistics-research/child-maltreatment.

Walters, S.B., Associates, Inc., 2010. Practical Kinesic Interview & Interrogation®. Public Agency Training Council.

Weston, P.B., Lushbaugh, C.A., 2006. Criminal Investigation: Basic Perspectives. Prentice Hall, Upper Saddle River, New Jersey.

Juvenile Cases

5

Juvenile Perpetrator Investigations

When reports of child abuse by alleged juvenile perpetrator (generally aged 12–17 years) occur, it is important to assess the severity and frequency of the abuse. These investigations are held to the same standard of proof (beyond a reasonable doubt) in the juvenile or family court as are those that move forward in the adult criminal court. Thus, the investigation should be handled in the same manner as cases with adult perpetrators. Interviews of juveniles responsible for abuse of another child or sibling must meet all the requirements of any standard law enforcement or child protection interview. In most states a juvenile officer or juvenile justice attorney will be required to be present, along with the alleged juvenile offender's parents to protect their rights. Just as in adult criminal cases, the multidisciplinary team (MDT) approach should be utilized. Alleged victims in these cases should be interviewed forensically, and the allegations should be investigated fully. When there is a concern of lack of supervision on the part of the parents in these cases, a coinvestigation involving child protective services (CPS) should be initiated immediately. As with adult criminal cases, CPS and law enforcement officers should share information regarding the allegations in accordance with state policy. When assessing family dynamics in the home, investigators should:

- Ensure the safety of the reported child and other children living in the home and address any ongoing risk of harm presented by the offending youth.
- Determine whether the maltreatment could have been reasonably prevented. Were the parents aware of the risk presented by the offender? Did the parents provide reasonable levels of supervision and control? Are the offending behaviors beyond what can be safely addressed in the child's home or does the child need to be removed even temporarily?
- CPS and/or the juvenile court should determine an appropriate treatment plan that will effectively address the offending behavior.

Child Abuse Investigation Field Guide.
Copyright © 2015 Elsevier Inc. All rights reserved.

Childhood Sexual Behavior Problems

Definition of Children with Sexual Behavior Problems

The Association for the Treatment of Sexual Abusers Task Force defines children with SBP as "children ages 12 and younger who initiate behaviors involving sexual body parts (i.e., genitals, anus, buttocks, or breasts) that are developmentally inappropriate or potentially harmful to themselves or others. Although the term sexual is used, the intentions and motivations for these behaviors may or may not be related to sexual gratification or sexual stimulation. The behaviors may be related to curiosity, anxiety, imitation, attention-seeking, self-calming, or other reasons (Silovsky & Bonner, 2003)."

(ATSA, 2006). Report of the ATSA Task Force on Children with Sexual Behavior Problems, p. 3).

There are several myths about children's sexual behaviors. Oftentimes, it is assumed that if a child exhibits concerning sexual behaviors, they themselves have been victims of sexual abuse. Although this may be the case, there are other factors that can contribute to their behavior. Dr. Toni Cavanaugh-Johnson categorizes children with sexual behavior problems into three categories: (1) sexually reactive, (2) children who engage in extensive mutual sexual behavior, and (3) children who molest. It is noted in her publication that the "children who molest" category is by far the smallest and will involve some degree of coercion. The first two categories will not. Factors that contribute to problematic sexual behaviors can include exposure to sexual information, abandonment, or maltreatment by trusted adults (Johnson, 2014).

"Children who molest should not be confused with adults who sexually offend" (Johnson, 2014). When a sexual act between two children occurs, it is common for investigative parties to label the initiator of the act as the perpetrator and the other child as the victim, which is the nature of the child protection/investigative process. Children labeled as the perpetrators are thought to have the propensity to continue to sexually offend, and will likely be treated as such by professionals, family, and peers. This is an unfair assessment.

Recent research shows that children with problematic sexual behaviors should not be labeled as perpetrators, but, rather, assessed by qualified mental health professionals and provided with proper treatment. Cognitive behavioral therapy is thought to be most effective.

"The key to modifying children's problematic sexual behaviors is to provide a health emotional, physical, and sexual environment with caring, consistent, and supportive caregivers" (Johnson, 2014).

When a report of sexual behavior between two children under the age of 12 years is made, it is important to work as an MDT. The key to addressing these behaviors is treatment, not punishment. Separating children from their families or labeling them as sex offenders at a young age will likely do more harm than good. Investigators should quickly determine if the behaviors are healthy and considered a part of natural sexual development (i.e., curiosity, gender exploration, looking, touching, but no penetration or "deviant" behavior).

If it is determined there are concerning behaviors that move beyond healthy sexual development, and the child is residing with other children who are at potential risk, responders need to immediately assess for possible contributing factors, such as boundaries in their home, family values about sexuality, history of abuse or neglect, and exposure to sexual material. Children involved in sexual behaviors should be interviewed in a safe, child-friendly environment, by a practitioner who is neutral, objective, and nonjudgmental. If there is access to a child advocacy center, a referral for a forensic interview would be appropriate, but the interview should be geared toward gathering information about the nature of the acts, in an effort to determine whether perpetration occurred. Inquiry regarding past sexual trauma is appropriate if conducted in a non-leading manner. Keep in mind, children with sexual behaviors act out for a variety of reasons, which are included in the list of contributing factors stated above. Other issues may also include poor parenting or a highly sexualized environment. When interviewing children, questions regarding their home life are valuable in assessing the origin of their behavior.

There may be instances when placement of the perpetrating child is necessary for the safety of other children. When considering these options, professionals need to keep in mind that treatment is of the utmost importance, and residential care should be the last resort. Residential facilities may increase the child's distress due to separation from family and community, as well as expose them to an entire population of children with problematic behaviors. Professionals should first consider family placement or therapeutic foster care, with treatment options readily available to the child, while offering a supportive, nurturing environment, with clear boundaries and increased supervision (ATSA, 2006).

References

ATSA, 2006. Report of the ATSA Task Force on Children with Sexual Behavior Problems. http://www.atsa.com/atsa-csb-task-force-report.

Johnson, T.C., 2014. Helping Children with Sexual Behavior Problems—a Guidebook for Professionals and Caregivers, fourth ed. Author, South Pasadena, CA.

Silovsky, J., Bonner, B.L., 2003. Sexual behavior problems. In: Ollendick, T.H., Schroeder, C.S. (Eds.), Encyclopedia of Clinical Child and Pediatric Psychology. Kluwer Press, New York, pp. 589–591.

Preparing for Court

6

Testifying in Court

Oftentimes, it is difficult for the public to believe that a parent of caregiver could harm a child. Juries are afraid of making mistakes and do not want to convict a parent or loved one of molestation of a child. Many jury members are parents themselves and can somewhat relate to the stresses of parenting and might believe that the caregiver "went a little too far" without malice or intent to harm the child. Studies have also shown that the public believes and wants to believe that the person who did this is "sick" or mentally ill. However, those same studies have shown that in the majority of cases, the person is not mentally ill at all. The National Center for Prosecution of Child Abuse has senior attorneys who are available to consult with the team, offer technical assistance, and can put the prosecutor in touch with other child abuse prosecutors around the country for additional support and advice.

When an investigation of child abuse leads to legal proceedings (grand jury, preliminary hearing, or criminal trial), investigators will be responsible for testifying about how the investigation was conducted. Timing of events is often an important factor. It is critical that all parties have to hand an accurate account of their part in the investigation. You may not be able to testify to what others did in the investigation, but you may need to give an overview and the court will then call each person to explain his or her actions. Make sure there are no gaps that are unexplained. Because your testimony will be essential in convincing a judge or jury that the investigation was thorough and reliable, you must present yourself as an experienced, competent professional. The following advice can help you accomplish that:

- *Be prepared.* Before being called to testify in any proceedings, make sure you know the facts of the case and what you will be expected to testify about. The prosecutor will usually meet with you before a trial to review your testimony and the facts of the case. If the prosecutor does not schedule such a pre-trial meeting, you should request one. The entire team that will be testifying should have all the case information and it should be consistent. Team members may very well have different pieces of the investigation, but the timeline and the

Child Abuse Investigation Field Guide.
Copyright © 2015 Elsevier Inc. All rights reserved.

charging documents should tell a complete and consistent history of events. In family court cases, the witnesses, if any, should have a pre-trial conference with the attorney. Each party must understand what is going to take place in the courtroom (Horsley, Testifying in Court). If a child is to testify it is imperative that the attorney meet with the child beforehand and explain what is going to take place. Identify people who will be in the courtroom and what their roles are. If the child will testify from a remote location or closed circuit TV, getting the child familiar with the surroundings is important. If the child or the parents or offender is intellectually, emotionally, or otherwise disabled, arrangements must be made to accommodate that person's special needs as well.

It is often helpful to organize your thoughts in a timeline fashion before testifying. Make a timeline with key points of information and be familiar with it. Ask to take it with you to the witness stand if you need to refer to it later. Anything you take to the stand can be examined and even read aloud in court. Be sure your notes only refer to the case you are testifying about and make sure there are no extraneous notes on the pages, for example, a grocery list, a phone number jotted in the margin, doodles on the page, and so on. Hornsby and Carlova, 1983 suggest the following examples:

- *Be truthful.* It may seem obvious that you should testify truthfully. However, defense attorneys will ask certain questions that can cause an investigator to become confused and hesitant to answer:
  - "Have you discussed your testimony with anyone before testifying today?" If you have discussed your testimony with the prosecutor, just say so. Most people in a courtroom know that good prosecutors spend time with their witnesses before trial. If the defense attorney implies that the prosecutor told you what to say, your answer should convey to the jury that the prosecutor's only instructions were for you to be truthful and accurate in your testimony.
  - "Isn't it true, detective, that you lied to my client during the interrogation?" If the defendant confessed during your interrogation, you can count on the defense attorney asking a question like this. Again, if you lied to the suspect, just say so. Lying to a suspect in the interrogation room is a common law enforcement technique and many legal precedents support the concept that deception is often necessary for effective law enforcement. Ideally, the prosecutor's follow-up questions will allow you to make it clear to the jury that you understand the difference between the need to deceive suspects in the interrogation room and the need to testify truthfully in the courtroom.
- *Review the case file.* Be thorough. Know exactly what the file does and does not contain. If necessary, ask the judge if you may refer to your notes before answering a question. Pay special attention to the chronology of events. Prepare a timeline of important events. You will be asked what you did,

when, and why. When you look at the crime scene photographs, try to picture yourself at the scene. You may be asked where various items were located in respect to others. Also, be sure to review all statements provided by witnesses and the defendant and be prepared to explain how those interviews were conducted (Horsley, Testifying in Court).

- *Appearance.* Dress in appropriate business attire or in uniform. Turn off your cell phone or pager. If you are a law enforcement officer, your duty weapon should not be visible (unless you are in uniform).
- *Never argue with the defense attorney.* The defense attorney will try to show that you did not conduct a professional investigation (which would mean that the defendant must be innocent). The attorney may use facial expressions, body language, and tough questions to accomplish this. Although your professionalism and integrity may be challenged, do not lose your composure. If you are disrespectful, unresponsive, or sarcastic, you will get in trouble with the judge and diminish the value of your testimony.
- *Be confident.* When appropriate, use positive terms that convey the conviction of your answer. Avoid using qualifying statements, such as "I think" or "I believe". If you know the answer, just give it. If you do not know the answer, say so. A common tactic for defense attorneys is to ask "If you had it to do over, could you have done a more thorough investigation?" If that is not true, say that you conducted a thorough investigation. Convey your confidence in the investigation and your professionalism to the jury.
- *Talk to the jury.* When asked a question look and listen to the attorney or judge asking it. Think about your answer for a moment and then, in most cases, look at the jury to explain it—especially if you are an expert witness. As an expert witness you are there as a friend of the court. You are not testifying for or against the defendant but are there to help the jury and the court understand something about your field of expertise. If you are a lay witness, you cannot give an opinion but are still there to convey some piece of information you have to the court. If it is a simple yes or no type of answer, look at the person asking the question and speak clearly so that the jury can hear. If it is an account of something, like "tell us what you did that night," take turns looking at the jury members individually if possible. The witness is there to tell the court something they know about. Therefore, talk to them like you were talking to a friend. Likeability is a huge factor in relating well to the jury. Deliver your testimony with confidence and sincerity.
- *Attend the final arguments.* During the trial, you probably will be allowed in the courtroom only when you testify. However, once the prosecutor and the defense rest their cases, you will probably be allowed to be present for the final arguments. Your presence tells the jury that you are interested in the outcome of the case. In addition, you can hear what both sides believe to be the strongest and weakest evidence in the case. This is an opportunity for you to learn what you did well and what you can improve on in your next investigation.
- *Talk to the prosecutor.* An excellent way to improve your courtroom testimony is to ask the prosecutor for feedback. In addition to providing personal

observations about your testimony, the prosecutor may be able to offer you suggestions for improvement for the next time you testify.

Special Note for the Attorney

- *Attorneys must accommodate disabilities.* One definition of disability is a medical, educational, or psychological condition that interferes with a person's ability to:
  - Speak, understand, and use language
  - Think and reason
  - Socialize, feel, behave
  - See, hear, move, and maintain health.

Disabilities can be physical, social or emotional, intellectual or of communication. Physical disabilities can be congenital or acquired and can be hidden or visible. They can be caused by injury, infection, or trauma. Remember that, often, people with physical disabilities understand and process information as well as people who do not have physical impairments. People with emotional problems are unable to manage feelings to control their behaviors. Sometimes they may need to wiggle and move about, and may need periods of silence. We know that children with emotional and social disabilities have the highest rate of abuse and neglect. Social/emotional disabilities are things like anxiety disorder, attention deficit and hyperactive disorder, bipolar disorder, depression, anger management, and many others. People with intellectual disabilities have difficulty with thinking and reasoning. This is often called "cognitive impairment."

It is very important to remember: When talking to parents the type of disability is the most important factor in determining what questions to ask and how to ask those questions.

If you can figure out what type of disability the child has, it will help you formulate a plan to work with them to be effective. When talking to them, talk slowly and plainly and go through the steps. Make eye contact. When working with the non-offending parent who has a disability or the child who has a disability, the prosecution must be flexible and must pose questions in a way that the person can understand them and respond accurately. Use common sense. Arrange the environment, as much as possible, for physical and emotional comfort. Explain what behavior is expected and why it is important. Be consistent. Use the same tone of voice and repeat important items as necessary until you are sure the person or child understands. It may be necessary to use visual, auditory, or tactile cues. If the person does not read well, simple sentences, not complex, will work better. Diagrams may be useful, or pictures. If the child or adult loses attention, find a way to redirect them back to the task at hand.

Have a plan … and a backup plan! The more you know about the parent's or child's particular disability, the better you can prepare to question him or her. Tailor your meeting to accommodate the person's needs. Be positive and be patient. Remember that a person or child is not defined by their disability. It is merely one area of weakness. Use the person's strengths to help you get the answers you seek.

Following are some simple suggestions that will assist the child in being prepared for the challenges of testifying (from: OJJDP CASA):

- Visit an empty courtroom and explain, using age-appropriate language, who will be in the court and their role in the proceedings.
- Give the child the opportunity to take various perspectives in the courtroom by allowing them to sit at the prosecutor's and defense counsel's tables, the judge's bench, and the jury box.
- Allow the child to sit on the witness stand and practice using the microphone.
- Practice answering general questions (not pertaining to the child's case) from the witness stand.
- Teach the child how to respond to confusing, misleading questions and what to do if the child does not know an answer.
- Have the child practice being sworn in (again, using age-appropriate language and if needed, visual tools, which can increase the perceived competency of the child).
- Explain courtroom-specific behaviors and terms, such as "objection," "overruled," and "please rise."
- Go over the difference between the truth and a lie.
- Give the child a realistic time frame of the court processes.
- Discuss how the child should act on the stand.

References

Hornsby, J.E., J.D., Carlova, J., 1983. Testifying in Court, second ed. Medical Economics Books, Oradell, NJ.

OJJDP - Court Appointed special Advocates (CASA) Downloaded 10/1//2014 from: http://www.casaforchildren.org/site/c.mtJSJ7MPIsE/b.8173513/k.1FB7/JP_10_NCAC.htm.

Resources

7

Glossary

Adjudicatory hearings held by the juvenile and family court to determine whether a child has been maltreated or whether another legal basis exists for the state to intervene to protect the child.

Adoption and safe families act (ASFA) signed into law November 1997 and designed to improve the safety of children, to promote adoption and other permanent homes for children who need them, and to support families. The law requires CPS agencies to provide more timely and focused assessment and intervention services to the children and families that are served within the CPS system.

Agency an entity with an administrative structure, most often a government, child placing, or regulatory entity.

Assessment the process used with the family to determine if the child has been abused or neglected and if intervention is needed to ensure child safety and reduce the risk of future abuse or neglect. The process includes, but is not limited to, what has traditionally been called an investigation, and it occurs throughout the life of the agency's involvement with the family.

Bed sharing a sleep arrangement in which an infant sleeps on the same surface, such as a bed, couch, or chair, with another person. Sleeping with a baby in an adult bed increases the risk of suffocation and other sleep-related causes of infant death.

Best practices recommended services, supports, interventions, policies, or procedures based on current validated research or expert consensus.

CASA court-appointed special advocates (usually volunteers) who serve to ensure that the needs and interests of a child in child protection judicial proceedings are fully protected.

Case closure the process of ending the relationship between the CPS worker and the family that often involves a mutual assessment of progress. Optimally, cases are closed when families have achieved their goals and the risk of maltreatment has been reduced or eliminated.

Case plan the casework document that outlines the outcomes, goals, and tasks necessary to be achieved in order to reduce the risk of maltreatment. An agreement, usually written, developed between the family, the child welfare worker, and other service providers. It outlines the tasks necessary by all individuals to achieve the goals and objectives to sufficiently reduce the risk of future child abuse and neglect.

Child Abuse Investigation Field Guide.
Copyright © 2015 Elsevier Inc. All rights reserved.

Case planning the stage of the CPS case process where the CPS caseworker develops a case plan with the family members.

Caseworker competency demonstrated professional behaviors based on the knowledge, skills, personal qualities, and values a person holds.

Central registry a centralized database containing information on all substantiated/founded reports of child maltreatment in a selected area (typically a state).

Certification a credentialing process in which the agency demonstrates compliance with and maintenance of minimum standards and requirements as part of a nongovernmental approval process.

Child Abuse Prevention and Treatment Act (CAPTA) the law (P.L. 93–247) that provides a foundation for a national definition of child abuse and neglect. Reauthorized in October 1996 (P.L. 104–235), it was up for reauthorization at the time of publication. CAPTA defines child abuse and neglect as "at a minimum, any recent act or failure to act on the part of a parent or caretaker, which results in death, serious physical or emotional harm, sexual abuse or exploitation, or an act or failure to act which presents an imminent risk of serious harm."

Child protective services (CPS) the designated social services agency (in most states) to receive reports, investigate, and provide intervention and treatment services to children and families in which child maltreatment has occurred. Frequently, this agency is located within larger public social service agencies, such as Departments of Social Services.

Collaboration a process of individuals and organizations in a community working together toward a common purpose. All parties have a contribution to and a stake in the outcome.

Concurrent planning identifies alternative forms of permanency by addressing both reunification and legal permanency with a new parent or caregiver if reunification efforts fail.

Confidentiality the protection of information obtained during a services intervention from release to organizations or individuals not entitled to it by law or policy.

Co-sleeping a sleep arrangement in which the parent (or another person) and infant sleep in close proximity (on the same surface or different surfaces) so as to be able to see, hear, and/or touch each other. Co-sleeping arrangements can include room sharing or bed sharing. The terms "bed sharing" and "co-sleeping" are often used interchangeably, but they have different meanings.

Cultural competence a set of attitudes, behaviors, and policies that integrates knowledge about groups of people into practices and standards to enhance the quality of services to all cultural groups being served.

Differential response an area of CPS reform that offers greater flexibility in responding to allegations of abuse and neglect. Also referred to as "dual track" or "multitrack" response, it permits CPS agencies to respond differentially to children's needs for safety, the degree of risk present, and the family's needs for services and support. *See also* Dual Track.

Dispositional hearings held by the juvenile and family court to determine the disposition of children after cases have been adjudicated, such as whether placement of the child in out-of-home care is necessary and what services the children and family will need to reduce the risk of maltreatment and to address the effects of maltreatment.

Disruption unplanned discontinuation of a child's placement with a foster or adoptive family.

Dual track term reflecting new CPS response systems that typically combine a non-adversarial service-based assessment track for cases where children are not at immediate risk with a traditional CPS investigative track for cases where children are unsafe or at greater risk for maltreatment. *See also* Differential Response.

Evaluation of family progress the stage of the CPS case process where the CPS caseworker measures changes in family behaviors and conditions (risk factors), monitors risk elimination or reduction, assesses strengths, and determines case closure.

Family assessment the stage of the child protection process when the CPS caseworker, community treatment provider, and the family reach a mutual understanding regarding the behaviors and conditions that must change to reduce or eliminate the risk of maltreatment, the most critical treatment needs that must be addressed, and the strengths on which to build.

Family foster care essential child welfare service for children and their parents who must live apart from each other for a temporary period of time because of physical abuse, sexual abuse, neglect, emotional maltreatment, or special circumstances. Children are placed in the homes of nurturing, licensed, trained caregivers.

Family group conferencing a family meeting model used by CPS agencies to optimize family strengths in the planning process. This model brings the family, extended family, and others important in the family's life (e.g., friends, clergy, or neighbors) together to make decisions regarding how best to ensure safety of the family members.

Family unity model a family meeting model used by CPS agencies to optimize family strengths in the planning process. This model is similar to the family group conferencing model.

Full disclosure CPS information to the family regarding the steps in the intervention process, the requirements of CPS, the expectations of the family, the consequences if the family does not fulfill the expectations, and the rights of the parents to ensure that the family completely understands the process.

Guardian ad litem a lawyer or lay person who represents a child in juvenile or family court. Usually this person considers the "best interest" of the child and may perform a variety of roles, including those of independent investigator, advocate, advisor, and guardian for the child. A lay person who serves in this role is sometimes known as a court-appointed special advocate or CASA.

Harm an injury received as a result of physical abuse, sexual abuse, neglect, or emotional maltreatment.

Home visitation programs prevention programs that offer a variety of family-focused services to pregnant mothers and families with new babies. Activities frequently encompass structured visits to the family's home and may address positive parenting practices, nonviolent discipline techniques, child development, maternal and child health, available services, and advocacy.

Immunity established in all child abuse laws to protect reporters from civil law suits and criminal prosecution resulting from filing a report of child abuse and neglect.

Initial assessment or Investigation the stage of the CPS case process where the CPS caseworker determines the validity of the child maltreatment report, assesses the risk of maltreatment, determines if the child is safe, develops a safety plan if needed to assure the child's protection, and determines services needed.

Intake the stage of the CPS case process where the CPS caseworker screens and accepts reports of child maltreatment.

Interview protocol a structured format to ensure that all family members are seen in a planned strategy, that community providers collaborate, and that information gathering is thorough.

Investigation an inquiry or search by law enforcement or CPS to determine the validity of a report of child abuse or neglect and to determine if a crime has been committed.

Juvenile and family courts established in most states to resolve conflict and to otherwise intervene in the lives of families in a manner that promotes the best interests of children. These courts specialize in areas such as child maltreatment, domestic violence, juvenile delinquency, divorce, child custody, and child support.

Kinship care formal child placement by the juvenile court and child welfare agency in the home of a child's relative.

Kinship foster care the daily parenting care of children by kin as a result of a determination by the court and the public CPS agency that a child must be separated from his or her parents because of abuse, neglect, dependency, abandonment, or special medical circumstances. In formal kinship care, the court places the child in the legal custody of the child welfare agency, and kin provide full-time care, protection, and nurturing.

Liaison the designation of a person within an organization who has responsibility for facilitating communication, collaboration, and coordination between agencies involved in the child protection system.

Licensing compliance with and maintenance of minimum standards and requirements that are defined by law and amplified by rules and regulations.

Such standards and requirements are aimed primarily at the protection of children and their parents but also offer protection to the agency in its assurance to the community that it meets these standards.

Mandated reporter individuals required by state statutes to report suspected child abuse and neglect to the proper authorities (usually CPS or law enforcement agencies). Mandated reporters typically include professionals, such as educators and other school personnel, health care and mental health professionals, social workers, childcare providers, and law enforcement officers. Some states identify all citizens as mandated reporters.

Multidisciplinary team established between agencies and professionals within the child protective system (CPS) to discuss cases of child abuse and neglect and to aid in decisions at various stages of the CPS case process. These terms may also be designated by different names, including child protection teams, interdisciplinary teams, or case consultation teams.

Neglect the failure to provide for the child's basic needs. Neglect can be physical, educational, or emotional. *Physical neglect* can include not providing adequate food or clothing, appropriate medical care, supervision, or proper weather protection (heat or coats). *Educational neglect* includes failure to provide appropriate schooling, special educational needs, or allowing excessive truancies. *Psychological neglect* includes the lack of any emotional support and love, chronic inattention to the child, exposure to spouse abuse, or drug and alcohol abuse.

Out-of-home care child care, foster care, or residential care provided by persons, organizations, and institutions to children who are placed outside their families, usually under the jurisdiction of juvenile or family court.

Parent or Caretaker person responsible for the care of the child.

***Parens patriae* doctrine** originating in feudal England, a doctrine that vests in the state a right of guardianship of minors. This concept has gradually evolved into the principle that the community, in addition to the parent, has a strong interest in the care and nurturing of children. Schools, juvenile courts, and social service agencies all derive their authority from the state's power to ensure the protection and rights of children as a unique class.

Physical abuse the inflicting of a non-accidental physical injury upon a child. This may include, burning, hitting, punching, shaking, kicking, beating, or otherwise harming a child. It may, however, have been the result of over-discipline or physical punishment that is inappropriate to the child's age.

Policies written requirements that direct business and service delivery practices of an agency. Policies should carry the approval of the agency's governing or advisory board.

Primary prevention activities geared to a sample of the general population to prevent child abuse and neglect from occurring. Also referred to as "universal prevention."

Procedures written guidelines developed by an agency's administration to ensure that operational practices are consistent with board-approved policies.

Protective factors strengths and resources that appear to mediate or serve as a "buffer" against risk factors that contribute to vulnerability to maltreatment or against the negative effects of maltreatment experiences.

Protocol an interagency agreement that delineates joint roles and responsibilities by establishing criteria and procedures for working together on cases of child abuse and neglect. Interagency agreements that delineate joint roles and responsibilities by establishing criteria and procedures for working together on cases in which child safety or family well-being is of concern.

Psychological maltreatment a pattern of caregiver behavior or extreme incidents that convey to children that they are worthless, flawed, unloved, unwanted, endangered, or only of value to meeting another's needs. This can include parents or caretakers using extreme or bizarre forms of punishment or threatening or terrorizing a child. The term "psychological maltreatment" is also known as emotional abuse or neglect, verbal abuse, or mental abuse.

Respite care temporary relief provided to caregivers to reduce stress, support family stability, prevent abuse and neglect, and minimize the need for a change in the child's placement.

Response time a determination made by CPS and law enforcement regarding the immediacy of the response needed to a report of child abuse or neglect.

Review hearings held by the juvenile and family court to review dispositions (usually every 6 months) and to determine the need to maintain placement in out-of-home care or court jurisdiction of a child.

Risk the likelihood that a child will be maltreated in the future.

Risk assessment to assess and measure the likelihood that a child will be maltreated in the future, frequently through the use of checklists, matrices, scales, and other methods of measurement.

Risk factors behaviors and conditions present in the child, parent, or family that will likely contribute to child maltreatment occurring in the future.

Safety absence of an imminent or immediate threat of moderate-to-serious harm to the child.

Safety assessment a part of the CPS case process in which available information is analyzed to identify whether a child is in immediate danger of moderate or serious harm.

Safety plan a casework document developed when it is determined that the child is in imminent or potential risk of serious harm. In the safety plan, the caseworker targets the factors that are causing or contributing to the risk of imminent serious harm to the child, and identifies, along with the family, the interventions that will control the safety factors and assure the child's protection.

Secondary prevention activities targeted to prevent breakdowns and dysfunctions among families who have been identified as at risk for abuse and neglect.

Service agreement the casework document developed between the CPS caseworker and the family that outlines the tasks necessary to achieve goals and outcomes necessary for risk reduction.

Service provision the stage of the CPS casework process when CPS and other service providers provide specific services geared toward the reduction of risk of maltreatment.

Sexual abuse inappropriate adolescent or adult sexual behavior with a child. It includes fondling a child's genitals, making the child fondle the adult's genitals, intercourse, incest, rape, sodomy, exhibitionism, sexual exploitation, or exposure to pornography. To be considered child abuse, these acts have to be committed by a person responsible for the care of a child (e.g., a babysitter, a parent, or a day care provider) or related to the child. If a stranger commits these acts, it would be considered sexual assault and handled solely by the police and criminal courts.

Substantiated an investigation disposition concluding that the allegation of maltreatment or risk of maltreatment was supported or founded by state law or state policy. A CPS determination means that credible evidence exists that child abuse or neglect has occurred.

Sudden infant death syndrome (SIDS) in some cases, the evidence is not clear or not enough information is available, so the death is considered to be "sudden infant death syndrome." This is a diagnosis of exclusion, and all other causes should be ruled out before this is the considered the cause of death.

Sudden unexplained infant death (SUID) the death of an infant younger than one year of age that occurs suddenly and unexpectedly. After a full investigation, these deaths may be diagnosed as:

Suffocation: When no air reaches a baby's lungs, usually caused by a block in the airway.

Entrapment: When a baby gets trapped between two objects, such as a mattress and wall, and cannot breathe.

Infection: When a baby has a cold or other infection caused by a virus or bacteria that makes breathing difficult.

Ingestion: When a baby takes something into the mouth that blocks the airway or causes choking.

Metabolic diseases: Conditions related to how the body functions that can lead to problems with breathing.

Cardiac arrhythmias: When a baby's heart beats too fast or too slow and affects breathing.

Trauma (accidental or non-accidental): When a baby experiences an injury.

Tertiary prevention treatment efforts geared to address situations where child maltreatment has already occurred with the goals of preventing child maltreatment from occurring in the future and of avoiding the harmful effects of child maltreatment.

Treatment the stage of the child protection case process when specific services are provided by CPS and other providers to reduce the risk of maltreatment, support families in meeting case goals, and address the effects of maltreatment.

Undetermined cause of death the death certification when the medical examiner or forensic pathologist does not know or cannot determine the cause of death. The case is still open and if and when new information is obtained a cause of death may be determined.

Universal prevention activities and services directed at the general public with the goal of stopping the occurrence of maltreatment before it starts. Also referred to as "primary prevention."

Unsubstantiated (not substantiated) an investigation disposition that determines that there is not sufficient evidence under state law or policy to conclude that the child has been maltreated or at risk of maltreatment. A CPS determination means that credible evidence does not exist that child abuse or neglect has occurred.

National Resources

These organizations offer training, technical assistance, and support to child abuse professionals:

American Professional Society on the Abuse of Children—www.apsac.org.

CornerHouse—www.cornerhousemn.org.

Gundersen National Child Protection Training Center—www.ncptc.org.

National Children's Advocacy Center—www.nationalcac.org.

National Children's Alliance—www.nationalchildrensalliance.org.

National District Attorneys Association—www.ndaa.org.

National Institute of Child Health and Human Development—www.nichd.nih.gov.

Office of Juvenile Justice and Delinquency Prevention—www.ojjdp.gov.

Office for Victims of Crime: Training and Technical Assistance Center—www.ovcttac.gov.

State Contacts (Alphabetically) and Resources for Reporting

These results are current as of May 7, 2014 Courtesy of *Child Welfare Information Gateway*. https://www.childwelfare.gov/pubs.

State toll-free numbers for specific agencies designated to receive and investigate reports of suspected child abuse and neglect.

Alabama

Toll Free: 800.422.4453.
http://dhr.alabama.gov/services/Child_Protective_Services/Abuse_Neglect_Reporting.aspx.

Alaska

Toll Free: 800.478.4444.
http://www.hss.state.ak.us/ocs/default.htm.

Arizona

Toll Free: (888) SOS-CHILD 888.767.2445.
https://www.azdes.gov/dcyf/cps/reporting.asp.

Arkansas

Toll Free: 800.482.5964.
http://humanservices.arkansas.gov/dcfs/Pages/ChildProtectiveServices.aspx#Child.

California

Toll Free: 800.422.4453.
http://www.dss.cahwnet.gov/cdssweb/PG20.htm.

Colorado

Toll: 303.866.5932.
http://www.colorado.gov/cs/Satellite/CDHS-ChildYouthFam/CBON/1251590165629.

Connecticut

TDD: 800.624.5518.
Toll Free: 800.842.2288.
http://www.ct.gov/dcf/cwp/view.asp?a = 2556&Q = 314388.

Delaware

Toll Free: 800.292.9582.
http://kids.delaware.gov/services/crisis.shtml.

District of Columbia

Toll: (202) 671-SAFE (202.671.7233).
http://cfsa.dc.gov/service/report-child-abuse-and-neglect.

Florida

Toll Free: (800) 96-ABUSE (800.962.2873).
http://www.dcf.state.fl.us/abuse/

Georgia

Toll Free: 800.422.4453.
http://dfcs.dhs.georgia.gov/child-abuse-neglect.

Hawaii

Toll Free: 808.832.5300.
http://humanservices.hawaii.gov/ssd/home/child-welfare-services.

Idaho

TDD: 208.332.7205.

Toll Free: 800.926.2588.

http://healthandwelfare.idaho.gov/Children/AbuseNeglect/ChildProtectionContactPhoneNumbers/tabid/475/Default.aspx.

Illinois

Toll Free: 800.252.2873.

Toll: 217.524.2606.

http://www.state.il.us/dcfs/child/index.shtml.

Indiana

Toll Free: 800.800.5556.

http://www.in.gov/dcs/2398.htm.

Iowa

Toll Free: 800.362.2178.

http://www.dhs.state.ia.us/Consumers/Test/ProtectiveServices.html.

Kansas

Toll Free: 800.922.5330.

http://www.dcf.ks.gov/Pages/Report-Abuse-or-Neglect.aspx.

Kentucky

Toll Free: 877.597.2331.

http://chfs.ky.gov/dcbs/dpp/childsafety.htm.

Louisiana

Toll Free: 855.452.5437.

http://dss.louisiana.gov/index.cfm?md=pagebuilder&tmp=home&pid=109.

Maine

TTY: 800.963.9490.

Toll Free: 800.452.1999.

http://www.maine.gov/dhhs/ocfs/hotlines.htm.

Maryland

Toll Free: 800.422.4453.

http://www.dhr.state.md.us/blog/?page_id=3973.

Massachusetts

Toll Free: 800.792.5200.

http://www.mass.gov/eohhs/consumer/family-services/child-abuse-neglect/

Michigan

Fax: 616.977.1154 or 616.077.1158.

Toll-Free: 855.444.3911.

http://www.michigan.gov/dhs/0,1607,7-124-5452_7119---,00.html.

Minnesota

Toll Free: 800.422.4453.

http://www.dhs.state.mn.us/main/idcplg?IdcService=GET_DYNAMIC_CONVERSION&RevisionSelectionMethod=LatestReleased&dDocName=id_000152.

Mississippi

Toll Free: 800.222.8000.
Toll: 601.359.4991.
http://www.mdhs.state.ms.us/fcs_prot.html.

Missouri

Toll Free: 800.392.3738.
http://www.dss.mo.gov/cd/rptcan.htm.

Montana

Toll Free: 866.820.5437.
http://www.dphhs.mt.gov/cfsd/index.shtml.

Nebraska

Toll Free: 800.652.1999.
http://dhhs.ne.gov/children_family_services/Pages/children_family_services.aspx.

Nevada

Toll Free: 800.992.5757.
http://dcfs.state.nv.us/DCFS_ReportSuspectedChildAbuse.htm.

New Hampshire

Toll Free: 800.894.5533.
Toll: 603.271.6556.
http://www.dhhs.state.nh.us/dcyf/cps/contact.htm.

New Jersey

TDD: 800.835.5510.
TTY: 800.835.5510.
Toll Free: 877.652.2873.
http://www.nj.gov/dcf/reporting/how/index.html.

New Mexico

Toll Free: 855.333.7233.
http://cyfd.org/child-abuse-neglect.

New York

TDD: 800.369.2437.
Toll Free: 800.342.3720.
Toll: 518.474.8740.
http://www.ocfs.state.ny.us/main/cps/

North Carolina

Toll Free: 800.422.4453.
http://www.dhhs.state.nc.us/dss/cps/index.htm.

North Dakota

Toll Free: 800.422.4453.
http://www.nd.gov/dhs/services/childfamily/cps/#reporting.

Ohio

Toll Free: 855.642.4453.
http://jfs.ohio.gov/ocf/reportchildabuseandneglect.stm.

Oklahoma

Toll Free: 800.522.3511.
http://www.okdhs.org/programsandservices/cps/default.htm.

Oregon

Toll Free: 800.422.4453.
http://www.oregon.gov/DHS/children/abuse/cps/report.shtml.

Pennsylvania

TDD: 866.872.1677.
Toll Free: 800.932.0313.
http://www.dpw.state.pa.us/forchildren/childwelfareservices/calltoreportchildabuse!/index.htm.

Puerto Rico

Toll Free: 800.981.8333.
Toll: 787.749.1333.
http://www2.pr.gov/agencias/adfan/Pages/AdministracionAuxiliardeProteccionSocial.aspx.

Rhode Island

Toll Free: (800) RI-Child 800.742.4453.
http://www.dcyf.ri.gov/child_welfare/index.php.

South Carolina

Toll: 803.898.7318.
http://dss.sc.gov/content/customers/protection/cps/index.aspx.

South Dakota

Toll Free: 800.422.4453.
http://dss.sd.gov/cps/protective/reporting.asp.

Tennessee

Toll Free: 877.237.0004.
https://reportabuse.state.tn.us/.

Texas

Department of Family and Protective Services.
Toll Free: 800.252.5400.
https://www.dfps.state.tx.us/Contact_Us/report_abuse.asp.
Spanish: http://www.dfps.state.tx.us/Espanol/default.asp.

Utah

Toll Free: 855.323.3237.
http://www.hsdcfs.utah.gov.

Vermont

After Hours: 800.649.5285.
http://www.dcf.state.vt.us/fsd/reporting_child_abuse.

Virginia

Toll Free: 800.552.7096.
Toll: 804.786.8536.
http://www.dss.virginia.gov/family/cps/index.html.

Washington

TTY: 800.624.6186.
Toll Free: 800.562.5624 or (866) END-HARM 866.363.4276. http://www1.dshs.wa.gov/ca/safety/abuseReport.asp?2.

West Virginia

Toll Free: 800.352.6513.
http://www.wvdhhr.org/bcf/children_adult/cps/report.asp.

Wisconsin

Toll Free: 800.422.4453.
http://dcf.wisconsin.gov/children/CPS/cpswimap.HTM.

Wyoming

Toll Free: 800.422.4453.
https://sites.google.com/a/wyo.gov/dfsweb/social-services/child-protective-services.

National Resource Agencies

Child abuse and neglect mandatory reporting state statute overview (Chart I)	
Category	**States**
Professionals mandated to report Current through April 2010	48 states, the District of Columbia, American Samoa, Guam, the Northern Mariana Islands, Puerto Rico, and the Virgin Islands list groups of individuals who are required to report suspected child abuse or neglect. New Jersey and Wyoming do not list specific groups of professionals. *Note*: Such individuals may include: Social workers, teachers and other school personnel, physicians and other health-care workers, mental health professionals, child care providers, medical examiners or coroners, and law enforcement officers. California, Connecticut, District of Columbia, Hawaii, Iowa, Illinois, Maine, Massachusetts, Nevada, Ohio, Vermont and Washington include coaches, camp/youth camp or residential camp personnel or owners, or recreational/sport program or facility personnel or administrators to report suspected child abuse or neglect (see each state for specific category of persons required to report).
Mandated reporting by other persons Current through April 2010	18 states and Puerto Rico: Delaware, Florida, Idaho, Indiana, Kentucky, Maryland, Mississippi, Nebraska, New Hampshire, New Mexico, North Carolina, Oklahoma, Rhode Island, Tennessee, Texas, and Utah. *Note*: Any person who suspects child abuse or neglect is required to report.
Reports are referred to law enforcement agencies when the alleged perpetrator is a person other than the parent or other caregiver Current through January 2009	9 states: Alaska, Connecticut, Florida, Iowa, Kentucky, Louisiana, Michigan, New Mexico, and Texas.

Cases which the suspected abuse is caused by someone other than a family member, or in which the abuse involves sexual abuse or severe injury to the child, are considered crimes and must be cross-reported to law enforcement agencies for investigation Current through January 2010	27 states: Alabama, Alaska, Arkansas, California, Colorado, Connecticut, Delaware, Florida, Georgia, Illinois, Iowa, Kentucky, Louisiana, Massachusetts, Michigan, Minnesota, Mississippi, New Hampshire, North Carolina, Oklahoma, Rhode Island, South Carolina, Texas, Vermont, Washington, West Virginia, and Wisconsin.
Penalties on mandatory reporters who knowingly or willfully fail to make a report when they suspect that a child is being abused or neglected Current through December 2009	47 states (Maryland, North Carolina, and Wyoming do not have statutes imposing penalties), the District of Columbia, American Samoa, Guam, the Northern Mariana Islands, and the Virgin Islands
Failure to report is classified as a misdemeanor Current through December 2009	39 states (Connecticut, Delaware, Massachusetts, Mississippi, New Jersey, Vermont, Virginia, and Wisconsin do not use this classification), American Samoa, Guam, and the Virgin Islands
Specify in the reporting laws the penalties for failure to report Current through December 2009	20 states (Alabama, California, Connecticut, Delaware, Florida, Louisiana, Maine, Massachusetts, Michigan, Minnesota, Mississippi, New Mexico, Rhode Island, South Carolina, Tennessee, Vermont, Virginia, Washington, West Virginia, and Wisconsin), the District of Columbia, Guam, the Northern Mariana Islands, and the Virgin Islands. *Notes*: Upon conviction, a mandated reporter who fails to report can face jail terms ranging from 10 days to 5 years or fines ranging from \$100 to \$5000.

From National Conference of State Legislatures (downloaded 2014).

Notes

Index

Note: Page numbers followed by "t" indicates tables.

O

P

R

S

9780128023273